ISO 9001
Audit Trail
A Practical Guide to Process Auditing Following an Audit Trail

ISO 9001
Audit Trail
A Practical Guide to Process Auditing Following an Audit Trail

David John Seear

AuthorHouse™
1663 Liberty Drive
Bloomington, IN 47403
www.authorhouse.com
Phone: 1-800-839-8640

First Published in March 2010

Second Edition published October 2012

Note:—The First edition was developed following a request to produce a practical guide to auditing following the publication of "Understanding the Audit Trail" published by IRCA Inform Issue 24 on the 10th December 2009.

http://www.irca.org/inform/issue24/Seear.html

A similar article is also in www.iso.org/tc176/ISO9001AuditingPracticesGroup

It is intended that Organisation, Certification Bodies and both Internal and External Auditors get the best out of the audit process to the benefit of their businesses.

This document is for all professional quality personnel and has been developed from the Original Back to Basics guidance documents used during auditor training. (Attached.) The attached guidance notes may be used as individual training notes to help Organisations improve.

© 2012 by David John Seear. All rights reserved.

No part of this book may be reproduced, stored in a retrieval system, or transmitted by any means without the written permission of the author.

Published by AuthorHouse   10/11/2012

ISBN: 978-1-4772-3489-1 (sc)
ISBN: 978-1-4772-3490-7 (e)

Any people depicted in stock imagery provided by Thinkstock are models, and such images are being used for illustrative purposes only.
Certain stock imagery © Thinkstock.

This book is printed on acid-free paper.

Because of the dynamic nature of the Internet, any web addresses or links contained in this book may have changed since publication and may no longer be valid. The views expressed in this work are solely those of the author and do not necessarily reflect the views of the publisher, and the publisher hereby disclaims any responsibility for them.

INDEX

Page	Section	Description
1		Index
3	1.0/1.1	Introduction/Historic Terminology
5	1.2	Reason Certification Introduced
7	1.3	Objective and Purpose
10/11	2.0/3.0	The Objective of the Standard/ Back to Basics
16	4.0	How to Prepare For the Audit
19	5.0/6.0	Starting the Audit/Auditing Primary and Secondary Processes
29	7.0	Product Realisation
61	8.0	Concerns
65	9.0	Summary of Simple Audit Flow
67	10.0	Conclusion
69	11.0	Original Back to Basics Guidance Documents
71	Part 1	Audit Trail
73	Part 2	Objective Evidence
75	Part 3	Specification
78	Part 4	Audit Criteria
80	Part 5	Random Sample
82	Part 6	Audit Findings
84	Part 7	Audit Evidence
86	Part 8	Competence
89	Part 9	Declaration of Conformity
93	Part 10	Certificate of Compliance
95	Part 11	Controlled Documents
97	Part 12	Certification
100	12.0	Final Thoughts
101	APPENDIX A	Sample Audit Plan
108	APPENDIX B	KEY Highlights
113	APPENDIX C	ISO 9000 Family of Standards (First 5 Pages)

1.0 Introduction

This is the second edition of "ISO 9001 Audit Trail" and the intention is to get **"Back to Basics"** and cover the importance of auditing the Primary and applicable Secondary Processes to ensure the specified requirements are being met. The first edition was produced following the publication of an article on "Audit Trail", which was developed by David John Seear and has been accepted by the ISO 9001 Auditing Practice Group (APG). It has also been highlighted in his letter in Quality World November 2009 and in a 700 word article published in the December 2009 issue of IRCA Inform, all of which address the topic and emphasises the importance of the "Audit Trail". This, the second edition, has been modified following a feed back request to include Secondary Processes and an example of auditing a service organisation. There have been only a small number of concerns over the general content of the first edition and therefore only minor clarification has been needed to improve the message and to illustrate how to audit a service organisation. This document has been developed to encourage audit improvement.

ISO 9001 is a tool—not an Objective. It is a tool for the Organisation to ensure that it has the systems in place to enable them to consistently provide a product/service that meets the specified requirements. It is also the criteria used by the Auditors to measure whether the Organisations have the Management System Requirements, Management Responsibilities, Resource Management, Product Realisation and finally the Measurement Analysis and Improvement in place to allow them to meet specified requirements and move forward.

KEY 1: REMEMBER ISO 9001 IS THE TOOL NOT THE OBJECTIVE

It is **NOT** the intention of this document to teach all the elements necessary to do a full professional audit, however the objective is to highlight the importance of a **"Process Audit** following an **Audit Trail"**. To achieve this, the document has targeted sections of ISO 9001 7.0 Product Realisation (Primary Process) referencing some sections of

4, 5, 6 and 8 (Secondary processes) and the relevant parts of sections 1, 2 and 3 that are often glossed over.

1.1 Historic Terminology

The first thing to remember, without going back into history too far, is that the forerunner to ISO 9001 namely BS 5750 existed before Quality System Certification was introduced. In fact certification was introduced using BS 5750 and came in three parts. BS 5750 Part 1 that covered Organisations that carried out design, Part 2 covered Organisations that did not do design and Part 3 was for Organisations that only did Final Inspection. This is, of course, a simplification of what was covered. However this approach allowed Purchasers to understand, from the type of certification given, what the Organisation was capable of doing.

The next thing to be aware of was ISO 9001: 2000 changed from a Purchasers standard to an Organisations standard.

The reason for this was prior to ISO 9001: 2000 the OLD terminology was:—
Purchaser----Supplier (Certified Organisation)----Sub-Contractor

When ISO 9001:2000 was introduced the NEW terminology became:—
Customer----Organisation (Certified Organisation)----Supplier

Note:—The new terminology in ISO 9001 2000 version above is missing in ISO 9001 2008. I would ask TC 176 to reconsider replacing it in the next issue of ISO 9001 2014? **Action TC 176**

The reason this was introduced in the year 2000 was because there was considerable confusion over the original "Supplier"—"Sub Contractor" Terminology. These original terms had been poorly taught and it was not unusual to find Supplier's (Old Terminology) stating they did not use sub contractors when it meant suppliers who provided any requirements needed for the production of the product. The old term

Supplier (Certified Organisation) was correct from a Purchaser's point of view because they were Supplier's to them.

The ISO 9001 standard is used in over 130 countries and as such it was more easily understood with the revised terminology as all Certified Organisations understood suppliers as being any one who supplied them.

This terminology, linked with the removal of ISO 9001 Part 2 and Part 3 reduced the benefit for the Purchaser. This meant it was no longer a Purchaser's standard and it weakened the quality of the information available to the buyer. (Customer).

Not withstanding the above, Independent ISO 9001 Certification should give Purchasers confidence that the organisations management system is able to consistently meet the specified requirements.

1.2 Reason certification was Introduced

The second thing to understand is why BS 5750 (ISO 9001) Certification was introduced. It was primarily introduced to stop or reduce multiple assessments. It was felt that an independent Accreditation Body approving Certification Bodies who in turn carried out Audits on Suppliers (Old Terminology) Organisations (Current terminology) would achieve this.

I will not go into the detail of why this was raised, however it was supported by the British Government as it was deemed <u>unnecessary</u> for British Industry to have numerous supplier audits taking place as it took up time, resources and in most cases was simple repetition as far as the Organisation (Current Terminology) was concerned.

Unfortunately, although this reduction in audits did occur, Purchaser confidence in Certification Audits has diminished and is now at an all time low and getting worse.

The Chartered Quality Institute position regarding third party certification to ISO 9001 has stated:

For purchasing organisations:

- **Third party certification to ISO 9001 is not a guarantee that a supplier will provide the quality of service or product specified by customers.**

Authors Comment It can be accepted that this is not something that can be guaranteed, however the certification body carrying out the audit should be auditing to see if the Organisation is capable of consistently providing products or services that meet the specified requirements. This is stated at the top of the next CQI paragraph below.

- **Third party certification to ISO 9001 should provide confidence that the supplier has a management system that is focused on consistently providing their customers with conforming products and services. However, there is still significant variation in the quality and value of third party certifications carried out by the various certification bodies across the world and for this reason some purchasing organisations have reduced confidence in ISO 9001 certification.**

Authors Comment

It is this lack of understanding of what ISO 9001 Certification is about that is the reason for developing this document highlighting the importance of the **AUDIT TRAIL** with the intention of improving the credibility of Internal Audits (1st Party), Vendor/Supplier Audits (2nd party) and Audits carried out by Certification Bodies (3rd Party).

The reason this situation has developed is mainly due to lack of understanding regarding what should be done during an Audit. There are some Auditors who believe that their role is to see if the supplier's management system complies with ISO 9001. This would be true if the scope clause 1.0 of ISO 9001 was recognised throughout the audit. Unfortunately this is ignored as many auditors are taught that only clauses 4-8 are relevant to an ISO 9001 Certification Audit.

In fact I have had not only auditors but trainers indicate that you don't need to know what the product/service is to do an ISO 9001 audit.

I have asked many times how is it possible to do a process audit and judge if the processes in place are capable of consistently providing the product that meets the customer and statutory and regulatory requirements (Scope) if you do not know what the output from the process should be?

It is important that all of the clauses in the standard should be considered especially the first three clauses as they are crucial to understanding the intention, purpose and scope of the standard. Even today sections 1-3 are barely touched on ignored or glossed over. It is this failure to recognise how to carry out a professional ISO 9001 audit and that is why audits have lost their credibility. The continued belief that the audit are to see if the organisations has a management system that meets the clauses 4-8 of ISO 9001 is not only wrong but illogical. This section of the book is intended to right that misconception.

KEY 2:—All audits should give the audited Organisation information about how robust their systems are in ensuring that they can consistently meet the required specification.

KEY 3:—It has been accepted that some Purchasing Organisations have reduced confidence in ISO 9001 Certification.

1.3 Objective and Purpose of ISO 9001

This brings us to the final important requirement and that is:—
The ISO 9001 Standard is a Tool Not an Objective. Yes you can have an objective to comply with ISO 9001 as long as that is understood to be meeting the intention of the first 3 clause not just clauses 4-8 of ISO 9001.

ISO 9001 Sect 1.1 General states:—
This International Standard specifies requirements for a quality management system where an Organisation:—

a) **needs to demonstrate its ability to consistently provide product that meets customer and applicable statutory and regulatory requirements** and
b) aims to enhance customer satisfaction through the effective application of the system, including processes for continual improvement of the system and the assurance of conformity to customer and applicable statutory and regulatory requirements.

In ISO 9001 "Product" is a generic term covering both Product and Service

There are also important notes

Note 1 In this International Standard the term "Product" only applies to

a) product intended for, or required by a customer
b) any intended output resulting from the product realisation processes.

Note 2 Statutory and regulatory requirements can be expressed as legal requirements

KEY 4:—The Statutory and Regulatory requirements called up in ISO 9001 clause 1.1a) are only those requirements that relate to the product/service itself.

The ISO 9001 standard is designed to provide a cross-reference to relevant clauses so that when applied sensibly to any Organisation's Management System it will ensure that the product can consistently meet the specified requirements.

KEY 5:—There is still a belief that certification audits are to see if the ISO 9001 Clauses 4-8 are covered within the organizations management system. This is incorrect as it conveys little or no information on how effective the processes are.

4-8 are covered within the Organisations Management System. This is incorrect as it conveys little or no information on how effective the processes are.

Introductory Conclusion

A) It is believed that unless Process Audits following an Audit Trail are reintroduced as standard practice there will be no improvement in the credibility of auditing and its ability to ensure the management system is capable of consistently providing product that meets customer and applicable statutory and regulatory requirements.
B) The Statutory and Regulatory requirements called up in ISO 9001 clause 1.1a) are only those requirements that relate to the product/service itself.

2.0 The Objective of the Standard

It is important to remember the original and still stated purpose of ISO 9001

The ISO 9001 2008 international standard specifies requirements for a Quality Management System where an Organisation:—

1.1 a) Needs to demonstrate its ability to consistently provide product that meets customer and applicable statutory and regulatory requirements.

To achieve this the processes must be audited following an AUDIT TRAIL to demonstrate the organisations ability to meet those requirements.

KEY 6:—From the above it is obvious that all auditing is about ensuring that the organisation can consistently meet the specified requirements.

3.0 Back to Basics

There are many "key" aspects to carrying out professional audits.

There is the need to **audit the process**, defined in ISO 9000 as:—

"**3.4.1 Process** set of interrelated activities which transforms **inputs into outputs**".

It is essential to fully understand the term Process when carrying out an Audit. A process is where you understand the input carry out an activity that then produces the desired output.

If the output of the process being audited is not understood then it is impossible to do a professional audit.

There is however a critical omission to these defined Terms and Definitions and that is "Audit Trail". This is one of the most important aspects of Auditing although it is not defined in ISO 9000:2005. It is this link between the two terms that enables the audit to be Professional.

KEY 7:—The failure to carry out a process audit following an audit trail is the single most important reason why audits are not effective

The reason this is important is simple, if you do not follow the process for a specific sample of orders or contracts that you know the required output for then it is not possible to carry out an audit that achieves the purpose and scope of ISO 9001. Lets take just one sample. It is relatively easy to look at what has been agreed (Specification) then follow the process though to ensure all the requirements are being met at each stage of the process. Once a sample is chosen there is no need to look at anything outside the sample/s being followed except for clarification. It is in fact simpler and easier to audit in this manner and more importantly it enables the auditor to judge if the management system being used is capable of consistently meeting the agreed requirements. Although this approach is used by some auditors, it is by no means universally accepted. It is this failure to ensure all audits, both internal and external, employ Process audits following an "Audit Trail" that undermines the credibility of audits.

In some cases the need to demonstrate that an audit has been carried out seems to be the objective. The benefit of the audit is compromised and in many cases the audit is a waste of time and effort.

Support for this approach would be strengthened if ISO 9000 had a definition for Audit Trail: Using the standard dictionary definitions for Audit and Trail the following definition can be arrived at.

KEY 8:—AUDIT TRAIL (Draft as no agreement has been reached)

An examination, by a qualified person, of an activity following the path that has been left by the process (See "Back to Basics Guidance documents" section in this book Part 1)

OR

A systematic approach to collecting evidence based on specific samples, that the output of a series of inter-related processes meets expected outcomes (APG version)

There are many quality professionals who have stated that it is not easy to write a definition for Audit Trail. There are others who state that Audit Trail is not applicable to ISO 9001 audits. Many ISO 9001 audits do not follow an Audit Trail and even when it is stated they do it usually means the trail of documents. This is incorrect because to carry out a professional audit the outcome of a specific process must be known or how can the auditor judge if the process is effective and can consistently achieve the desired output?

PROCESS

The first thing to be clear about is what is a process?
Following feedback on the Audit Trail article it is clear some people believe the process is the way the procedures are set up and followed during the audit. **This is NOT true.**

The process is how something is achieved.

The standard identifies a process as:—

INPUT ⟶ ACTIVITY ⟶ OUTPUT

This is a good start, however the term INPUT must include what is required. In other words it needs to specify what the requirements are otherwise it is not possible for the OUTPUT to be checked to see if it meets the Specification.

This specification is the "KEY" to all auditing activity.

If it is not known what is required it is not possible for the auditor to assess the process to see if it is capable of providing a consistent product or service that meets the specification.

The final part of this is the ACTIVITY between the Input and Output and this is what the auditor audits. Professional Auditors will always understand what is required (Specification) for each process they audit and will then, using ISO 9001 clauses, evaluate the ACTIVITY to see if it is adequate to consistently achieve the specification that is required.

What is an Audit Trail?

As explained in the definition it allows the PATH used by the process to be examined to judge if what takes place is able to consistently achieve the required output:—

a) A simple example of this could be that the Organisations purchase order being audited requires a Material Certificate for a bought in item. When the Auditor asks to see this Certificate they can only offer an alternative as they can't find the one for that particular order. This is of course not acceptable as the TRAIL being followed requires the certificate for the specific order being followed. Even if they had the correct certificate there is more for the auditor to do, how do they control the certificate? How is it received, identified and stored? Does it retain its link to the product it self? If it needs to be passed to the Customer how is this managed? What records are kept? The <u>Audit Trail</u> approach would follow this process through to ensure it is consistently controlled and applied.

b) You are auditing a Main Car Dealers Servicing department from taking the order for a car to be serviced to returning the car fully serviced to the required service level. In this process a sample of cars being serviced are chosen as the representative sample. These are chosen at the start of the audit and the process for servicing these cars will be followed. You would include a car nearing completion plus others as time allows. You would obtain the job numbers or car numbers to identify how the work has been scheduled. The next thing to check what service was required. Was the service agreed with the customer, does this match the mileage, what was the previous mileage and date of service? Check if the service chosen is correct by checking the service level chosen (10k-20k-40k etc.) Identify what information the Organisation has on what is required for each service. How is this document controlled is it a formal manufacturers standard service level (Check-list) for each of the recognised service levels or is it just their own version. If it is there own version how was this devised where did the information come form? How do they ensure they have the latest version of this document? Were there any extra requirements that the customer had advised the organisation of? How are these requirements passed to the Technician carrying out that service. How are the spares passed to the Technician. Can the spares issued be cross-referred to the spares fitted and can they be identified as the actual spares taken from the store. Is this stock or has it been ordered in. Go through the actual material used and verify that this is correct for that make and that version of car. Throughout this process you check the procedures/ work instructions etc to see if the process would ensure the requirements are met, however the audit is not just to see the documented process is being followed but the process itself is robust and would indeed ensure the correct information is available. This only covers part of what is required as it has not even touched on the actual work being carried but hopefully it illustrates what is expected from a professional audit. Remember the audit is NOT just auditing to see if the procedures are being followed but checking to see if the process being used is able to consistently achieve the required outcome.

> *Without taking it further these examples are to show how the process is followed ensuring that all the linked activities for each chosen sample is, when audited, able to objectively demonstrate that the Management System being used can consistently meet the specified requirements. From now on the auditing example will be for a motor dealers organisation.*

Note:—The term "Management System" does not mean "Documented System". An effective management system may just require competent people with no procedures.

4.0 How to Prepare For the Audit

The scope and the time frame for the audit is normally specified by the person requiring the audit (The Originator). The objective of the audit should also be defined. The first task is to make contact with the Organisation/s giving them a rough time scale e.g. sometime in August 2012. This is especially important where there are a number of Organisations being audited in a country or at different locations.

Once contact has been made with the auditee's Organisation, the "Contact" the Auditor will be dealing with will be identified. It is this person that will act as the liaison with the Auditor. The initial information needed will include:—

- What is the normal working week and do they work shifts?
- What is the start and finish times for the day and shift workers?
- What are the times for lunch and are there set times for any breaks in the day?
- Does all the work take place at this location? Are there other locations?
- Will access be available to all areas? (Secret or Confidential)
- Any safety requirements (Can they provide PPE)?
- Where they are located, how easy is it to get to them and best route?
- Plus any other information the auditor may need.

4.1 Audit Programme:—

ISO 9000 (3.9.2) set of one or more audits planned for a specific time frame and directed towards a specific purpose.

The above information is needed to organise this programme and the time needed to develop this should not be underestimated especially if it involves different countries, flights, hotels etc. The programme in simple terms is on what days will Organisations be audited taking into account travel arrangements.

Note to Auditor WHEN PLANNING AND CONDUCTING THIS TOUR THERE MAY BE ADDITIONAL FACTORS TO CONSIDER eg: political/security issues, culture, health hazards and reduced safety standards.

AUDIT PROGRAMME FOR TRIP TO   XXXXXX

AUDITOR   Luke Around   DATE: 13th-18th XXXX

		Enter details of chargeable days						
Date	Days	Company + Mancode Or Location(s)	Activity			Travel Details		
			Travel	Audit	Other (specify)	Mode	Depart	Arrive
13		Manchester—Dublin	X			Flight	0800	0855
13		Dublin—Galway	X			Car	10.00	13.00
14	1	Company A Galway		X				
15	1	Company B Shannon		X				
16		Shannon—Dublin	X			Car	18.00	23.00
17	1	Company C Dublin		X				
18	1	Company C Dublin		X				
18		Dublin—Manchester	X			Flight	20.50	21.40

It should be noted that the scope of the audit and the number of audit days should be given as soon as contact is made. On agreement an Audit Plan should be set up:—

4.2 Audit plan:—

ISO 9000 (3.9.12):—Description of the activities and arrangements for the audit.

This will be a document that indicates the start time and activities that will take place. It usually covers departments and timings only. It normally follows the process in a structured manner that enables the auditor to follow the activities sequentially.

It should be noted that the Plan is following the process <u>NOT</u> the ISO 9001 clauses.

The attached Audit Plan **(See Appendix A)** is a simplified summary running through the audit process demonstrating how to link the plan to an Audit trail.

All auditing whether they are 1st Party, 2nd Party or 3rd Party should ensure that the process is able to consistently achieve the specified requirements. The Internal audit process should, if it is to be beneficial, include interfaces between departments. Each Internal audit normally covers a small part of the full process.

It is important that Internal Audits should also be an audit of the process following an Audit Trail and this requires the auditor to have knowledge of what each process should achieve.

Management may also include Internal Audits that are not directly related to the product or service provided. These Audits can also be carried out against ISO 9001 requirements however they should not be directly audited by Certification bodies whose primary auditing role is to see if the Organisation can consistently meet the product specification.

Audits that are solely planned against the clauses of ISO 9001 are NOT effective in demonstrating compliance with the specification.

5.0 How to Start the Audit

Auditors should always remember why the audit is taking place. The primary purpose of an audit is to ensure that the processes being audited are capable of consistently meeting the specified requirements. It should be noted it is impossible for a 2nd or 3rd Party auditor to carry out a Professional Audit of an Organisation unless the auditor takes the time to understand the specification of the product/service required including any statutory and regulatory requirements that relate to the product/service itself. It is this Professional approach to Auditing that allows the auditor to identify the strengths and weaknesses in the process and decide if that Organisation is capable of consistently meeting those specified requirements.

Internal audits should also follow an audit trail, however the audit scope is normally just a small part of the overall process. All of these audits need the auditor to know what the requirements are for the process being audited and should verify that the process with its controls and systems is able to achieve those requirements.

Note: A good approach is to use a form that captures all the names and roles of everyone seen during the audit. It should also identify who attended the opening and closing meeting. (This is useful information when, towards the end of the audit, the training records are checked as this enables personnel from the list to be sampled and checked against the activities they were actually seen doing during the audit.)

Opening Meeting

An opening meeting is always carried out this is to go over what has been discussed during the planning and is the opportunity to explain what the audit is about. The opening meeting is intended to set the scene for the audit and explain the approach that will be taken:—

- Introductions
- Confirmation of scope and objectives

- Confirm the Audit Plan is still acceptable (Should be sent and agreed before the audit)
- Ensure timings are still suitable
- Any "Special" concerns that could affect the audit. Fire drills, Management meetings etc
- It gives the opportunity to remind the meeting attendees what you are there to achieve. You advise them that you are their to help identify the good practices as well as identify whether there are any weaknesses in their system.
- You confirm the time of the closing meeting and confirm how the findings will be reported at the end of the meeting
- Then give all attendees the opportunity to ask any questions they may have.

Note: people are often nervous your role is to ensure they understand you are there to help.

6.0 How to Audit

It is important to prepare an Audit Plan that is given to the organisation prior to the visit for their review and to give them an idea which departments you will be visiting and when. Please refer (Appendix A) at the back of this part of the book for an example of an Audit Plan. Professional Auditors will normally do a walk through the plant to see the location of the departments and visit the area where the finished article, product or service is being finalised ready for despatch. This enables the auditor to see what's actually taking place and at that time identify job or contract numbers that are being worked on. From this information it is an easy task to go back to the service reception area and identify the agreed requirements for that specific product or service. This is the starting point and allows relevant samples to be chosen, in the case of a car service the cars identity so that the process can be checked to ensure what takes place is controlled and will meet the service requirements. Once a selective sample of car servicing has been identified this will form the start point of the audit. Example used to demonstrate this audit approach is "Top Down" after having identified and chosen a number of samples from the walk around.

From this starting point the "Audit Trail" is selected and followed through. It is normal to take a sample. The term, "Random Sample" is often used by auditors, however, it is better to use "Selective" or "Representative Sample" as this is what is actually meant. (See Guidance note Part 5 Random Sample).

For a 2nd party audit this means identifying a similar or identical product to the product or service that is required. For a third party Auditor it means the product identified in their Certified scope noting any exclusions. This is therefore NOT a totally Random Sample.

For internal audits it is what is happening at that time.

When the samples have been chosen (Note:—one is not normally considered a suitable sample). The minimum suggested is three but can be more, however, it does of course depend on the number of days (Time) allowed for the audits and it is not always possible to follow all chosen samples through from beginning to end. It also depends on the complexity of the product or service being provided and the scope of the audit given as this may only cover one contract. It is important to realise that samples are taken throughout the auditing process e.g. Purchase Orders sampled must relate to that particular job (Contract) and the number chosen is up to the auditor. The number of samples chosen should be sufficient to enable the auditor to be confident that the system is working, or not.

Primary and Secondary Processes

Feed back from the First Edition of the March 2010 Audit Trail book indicated that there was little mention of Secondary Processes.

So lets look at both the Primary process and the Secondary support processes in more detail as they will be included in the example used to show how a process audit following an audit trail is carried out.

In some Organisations they have more than one Primary Process especially if they make different products or provide different services.

In fact the main Objective of ISO 9001 is to give confidence to both the organisation and the Customer that their management system is robust and can consistently meet the required specification. In this example as already explained we will concentrate on car servicing and ignore any other activity such as car sales.

Primary Process

The ISO 9001 standard requires Organisations to:—

- Determine the Processes and their application throughout the Organisation ISO 9001 (ISO 9001 4.1.a)
- Determine their sequence and interactions (ISO 9001 4.1 b)
- Determine the criteria and methods of control (ISO 9001 4.1.c)

- Include a description of these in the Quality Manual. (Normally Primary)

This primary process is normally covered in ISO 9001 clause 7 Product Realisation ably supported by the secondary processes as appropriate.

Organisation often develop high level flow charts that are used to illustrate the primary processes although actually using a flow charts is not an ISO requirement as a simple list of activities that follow the process is equally acceptable. It is up to the Organisation to decide what is most appropriate.

The primary process is the process that is used to ensure that the product or service meets the specified requirements by using a Quality Management System (QMS) that controls the process in a consistent and effective manner.

Primary Processes will be covered in more detail a little later but let us look at an example of a Primary process:—

1. **Approved Supplier List (7.4.1)**
   This activity can be considered a Primary Process.
   The reason the Approved Supplier List (ASL) has been chosen is because this area is often poorly audited. The purpose of the audit is not to see if they have an approved supplier list and tick it off the list of requirements but to see if the process used in developing this list can give information on the credibility and the reliability of the suppliers or contractors being used. Once again, in good audit style, a sample of suppliers or contractors are chosen linked to the relevant sample of jobs chosen on the "Walk Around" or from the list of jobs going through that day. There is no point just looking at any item bought in from a supplier as you need to link this to the sample of cars that were chosen. From this information it should be possible to check that they suppliers being used were on the ASL and if so, what criteria were used to put them there? If it is as a result of previous good supply—check some evidence, or if it is as a result of supplier audit—have a look at the audit report. Lets face it

using a poor supplier or contractor can have a significant effect on the ability to meet the customer's requirements. One of the most significant problems experienced here is that if there is no information on the individual suppliers listed on the ASL it can invariably lead to orders being placed with the lowest bidder. Historical record on past performance is a powerful indication of whether a supplier can meet the specified requirements and where it is "weighted" this can be used in the decision making process.

The information supporting the ASL can be in the form of:—

General Supplier/Vendor information

- Are they ISO 9001 certified and is the certificate valid?
- Who is the Certification and Accreditation Body?
- What is the scope of their certification
- Does it cover the intended supplier/contractor location?
- Is there supplier capability questionnaire available?

For previously used suppliers:—

- Was previous orders delivered in time?
- Did the previous orders meet the specified requirement?
- Did your Organisation have to inspect the goods on receipt?
- Have any items from that supplier been rejected
- Were there any price variations?
- Etc

If the Organisation does not have information on the Contractor or Supplier that can be used in the bid analyses process then, as already stated, it puts into doubt the validity of the decision making process.

Secondary Processes

Secondary Processes are not specifically mentioned except by clause requirements outside ISO 9001 section 7 but they normally support the Primary Process. These Secondary processes are too many to list and are, in effect, any activity that supports the Primary Processes.

Let us look at an example of a Secondary process:—

2.0 Human Resources (6.2)

A good technique as already mentioned is to make a note of the individuals seen during the audit of the Primary Process and what each individual was doing (Job Role). From this list of personnel a sample is taken (see guidance note Part 5 Random Sample) and determine how the competence of those personnel was established. The sample taken can be then judged against what they were actually seen doing and in this way checking if competent personnel were employed at those stations. This takes in training or other actions to demonstrate competence and the effectiveness of the actions taken. It is important, in this process, to ensure appropriate records of education, training, skills and experience are developed and maintained. Once again to do this effectively it is necessary to audit the process that is being used to judge how effectively this is controlled and managed. This is carried out by following an audit trail to demonstrate that the personnel from the sample chosen are competent to do what they are being asked to do. An additional check of their competence may be carried out by checking the likes of non-conformance records and customer complaints to see if there is any correlation between their activities and if this can be linked to lack of competence of any individuals.

As previously indicated it is not the intention here to go through every primary or secondary process but it is hoped that the above examples will go some way towards explaining how auditing may also include secondary processes that directly impact or support the Primary Process. It again emphasises the importance of auditing a process following an Audit Trail. It also emphasises the importance of taking relevant samples and following those samples through to ensure that the system in place can consistently achieve the required outcome.

Other processes

It should be recognised that there are also activities that are not directly primary processes or even secondary processes that are used to support the primary process. These activities are often looked at right at the beginning of the audit after the opening meeting (See Appendix A Audit Plan).

They include the areas covered by Management Responsibility and Measurement, Analyses and improvement where they are not **directly** related to either the primary or secondary processes E.g:—

5.3 Quality policy
5.4 Quality objectives
5.6 Management review
8.2.2 Internal Audit etc

These activities are important for management to improve, control and direct the organisation and get everyone all pulling in the same direction. They often allow the auditor to see how well management understand the benefits of the ISO 9000 Family of Standards (FoS).

A1 Example of a simple basic Car Servicing Process Map

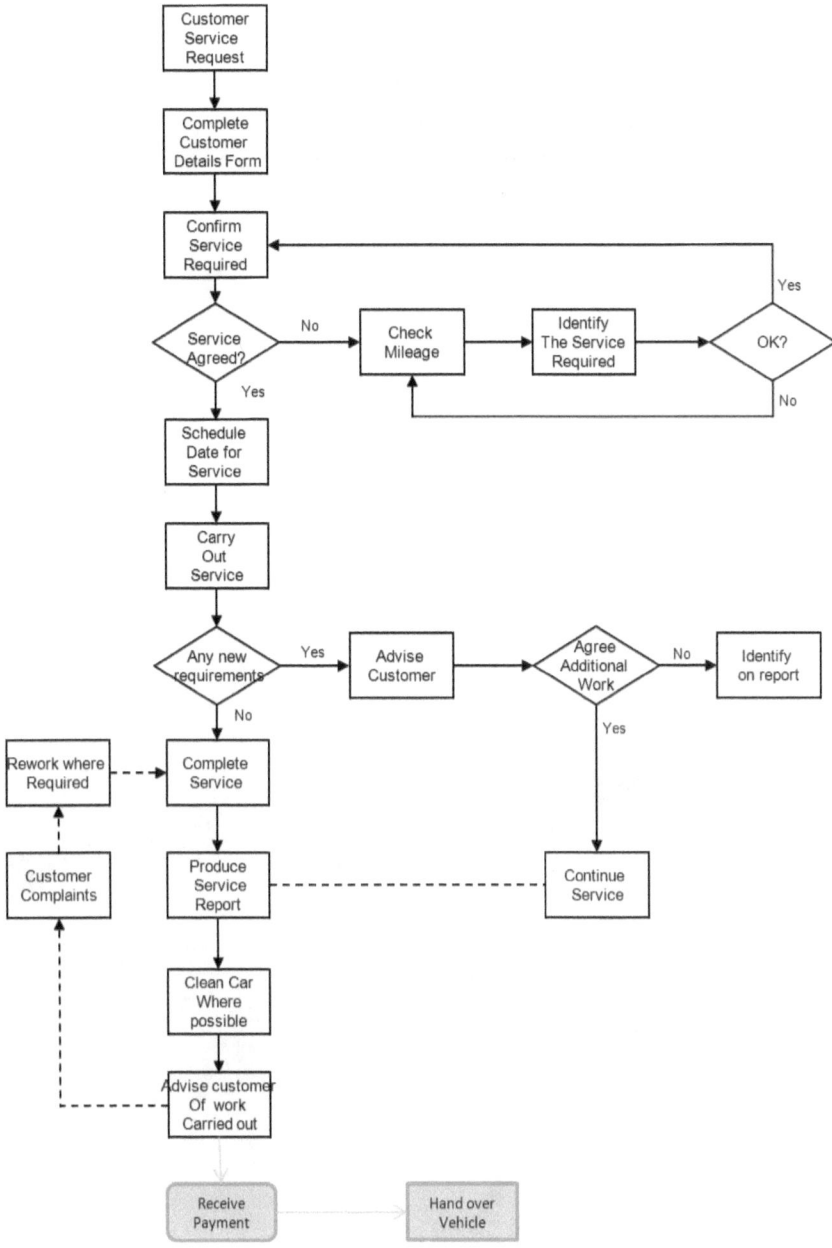

The basic car servicing flowchart will be used to demonstrate a process audit.

As already explained the technique, if you do not know the layout and departments of the organisation you are auditing, is to do a "Walk About" following as far as is practical the primary process. During this "Walk About" notes are made of the jobs that are going through at that time including what is scheduled to go through.

7.0 Product Realisation ISO 9001:2008 Section 7

There are many ways of tackling an audit however there is one method that should not be used and that is auditing by ISO 9001 clauses. The only effective audit is a process based audit where the auditor knows what the output should be for each process and is able to judge if the management system in place is able to consistently meet the specified requirements. Some people seem to believe that the management system is having a documented system and this is incorrect. A quality management system (QMS) covers everything that the organisation needs to meet the customer requirements. The organisations management is responsible for deciding what is needed to run the business not the Certification Body. It is not necessary to have every activity that is carried out supported by a procedure or other documented requirement. Management decide what documents are required.

KEY 9:—When auditing against ISO 9001 it is not the clauses that are being audited but the process.

Throughout the audit the auditor will use many different clauses at any point during the process audit. The start of the process, as already explained, is to identify your sample of Contract/s or Order number/s. When these have been identified the audit trail can begin. The biggest mistake auditors make is to think they are only auditing to see if procedures are being followed. Do not misunderstand what has just been written, procedures, work instructions, check lists and all the management systems are crucial to the ability to achieve customer satisfaction and as such are very important. In fact these, together with Competence and Resource Management are the tools that enable Organisations to consistently achieve the specified requirements. The point being made is, as important as they are, the purpose of the Audit is about whether the Organisations management system can consistently achieve the requirements of the Customers contract or order.

It is not about checking if the clauses of ISO 9001 are covered within the quality management system. As already stated the ISO 9001 standard is a tool not an Objective. There are five main clauses (4-8) within the ISO 9001 standard that are used to compare what is taking place with what is required. There are a further 23 sub clauses. Of these sub clauses at least 18 may be applicable anywhere within the audit process. Any of these clauses may be called up when a non-conformity has been found.

An example of some clauses that may be used at any point throughout the Auditing Process are:—Control of Documents, Control of Records, Responsibility and Authority, Competence and Training, Infrastructure and Work Environment to name a few.

Note:—The term contract will be used for the customer order

The first step and the one that is so often missing is to understand what the Contract requires. This review of the contract is the "Key" element to Professional auditing.

It is proposed in this example to use the **servicing organisation** of a main car dealers organization, as most readers will be familiar with this activity. This Organisation can be considered providing a service rather than a Product. ISO 9001 covers this in Section 3 Terms and Definitions where it states that wherever the term "Product" occurs, it can also mean "Service.

Note:—Professional audits will always identify good things as well as things of concern as that gives a balanced view. Too many auditors only look for what is wrong and this can be counterproductive and unfair.

The positive and negative Audit Evidence is gathered from each part of the audit activity throughout the process.

It is not normally necessary to take photo copies of the Objective Evidence seen as the formal note taking is usually sufficient to identify what was seen and whether it was acceptable or not. (See Back to Basics 2 Objective Evidence)

The auditor should now have a number of contracts (Car servicing) that can be used to verify that the process is in control. Other appropriate samples may be taken as the audit progresses.

The audit will now take place based on the car service process map

As already explained earlier in section 6 it is a good idea to see what is taking place at that time by doing a walk around the Organisation and making notes of cars already in or awaiting service. This is followed by a detailed look through the relevant documents used including any procedures, work instructions, check lists, drawings, any applicable national standards such as testing (MOT in the UK) and even product standards to select a few important requirements.

The things that should be noted and may come from any part of the requirements are:—

- The list of the cars scheduled for service during the audit.
- The relevant procedures and forms used for registering a car for servicing
- Any procedures, work instructions, forms, check lists etc being used.
- The vehicle mileage and registration number
- The recommended service schedule relating to the mileage.
- Any other special requirements the owner wants looked at
- How they agree the date and time for the service
- The details of the owner name address and agreed time frame for the service
- The owners contact details (Important if other work is identified)
- Pick up time
- The relevant service check list for that car at that mileage or frequency
- Previous service history

Please be aware the above is an example. As can be seen it can be anything that is specified within the contract. It is not the auditor's role to check everything and this is where selective sampling comes

in. (Back to Basics No 5 Random Sampling). It is not the intention to cover everything that needs to be carried out, as that would make this document too wordy and difficult to follow. The intention is to give sufficient examples so that the basic concept of auditing a process following an audit trail are understood

There is no simple way of deciding what should be chosen. This is where the auditors eyes and ears pick up and identify anything that would enable them to ensure that the Organisation has identified the requirement and that these requirements have been passed on through the realisation process to the people who have to do the work.

It is this skill of the auditor that enables them to pick out relevant "Key" requirements that will ensure a professional audit.

CAR SERVICE REQUEST

After the "Walk Around" a visit is made to the Customer service department to understand how each car is registered for service. You look at all the documents that are used and take a sample of the jobs that are scheduled during the days of your visit. The control of documents is then considered. **(Clause 4.2.3)** Are they controlled or uncontrolled (See Guidance Document 11) Make a note of the title of the documents, date and issue status. If it's a form its specific identify. Also look to see what records are kept, where and for how long. **(Clause 4.2.4)** These two clauses are applicable at every location that is visited.

The information that is held within these documents should let the auditor see how it is controlled and how effective it is as it covers what the customer requires. **(Clause 7.2)**

COMPLETE CUSTOMER DETAILS FORM

The sort of things you look for is how well they capture the customer's requirements. Does it give all the information you would expect it to obtain. Check document control and issue status. **(Clause 4.2.3)**

Remember you are there to see if the process is effective not just to see if they are following their procedures. You may even ask who deals with customer complaints and ask if they get many complaints. **(Clause 8.2.1)** make a note of this and who controls this **(Clause 5.5)**. The information obtained may cover the reason why the customer requires a service. Is it time based or mileage based. How do they decide what needs to be done.

CONFIRM SERVICE REQUIREMENTS

The organisation should obtain agreement of the service required and ensure any problems the customer may have with the car have been identified. **(Clause 7.2)**
The customer may have non-standard work that needs attention:—

- There could be special requirements to examine the brakes as they pull to one side.
- There is a leak on the engine somewhere that is marking the customers drive.
- This is an agreed extended service that uses longer oil filters to extend the time between services
- Any special tolerances such as valve clearances
- Specific oils and greases required
- Minimum thickness remaining on brake pads before they are changed
- Specified clearances or allowable movement on specific equipment

The auditor may even look out for one or more contracts that have other work required that is not just a standard service to see how this is handled. In fact it is normal to take the sample based on different service requirements.

Once all the requirements of the customer have been captured it is important to see how the organisation decides when the service can take place. What information do they have to ensure there is the capacity to do the work on the proposed day? Who has the responsibility for this activity? **(Clause 5.5.1)** It is important to make a note of all the people you meet during the audit and their roles so their training records can be looked at later in the audit. **(Clause 6.2.2)**

SERVICE AGREED

When the customer requirements are fully understood and the date and time for the car to be bought into the garage has been confirmed and possibly the price agreed the process for this has to be examined to see if it is effective. This should be recorded as this is the agreed contract. (Clause 7.2.2) If there is some disagreement then the process for justifying the type of service proposed, cost and the time and changes are reviewed until it is resolved. When it is the process goes back to "Confirm service required" and obtain customer agreement.

SCHEDULE DATE FOR SERVICE

The date of the service and any extra service offered are formalised. E.g Car loan to customer? Run the customer to where they want to be and possibly delivery of car to customer after the service. Check how these arrangements are captured to ensure they are delivered.

CARRY OUT SERVICE

This now gets into production and service provision **(Clause 7.6).**
The importance of having a sample of vehicles to follow will become evident at this point.

The purpose of an audit is to follow the same order right through the process from receipt of vehicle through to return of the vehicle to the owner. That is what ISO 9001 scope and purpose covers. The first thing needed will be whatever document is passed down to the technician servicing the car. It might be a standard service sheet for that mileage. E.g. 20,000 mile service. The auditor will check the document title, number, issue and date of this document. This information will be written down as this is objective evidence (See Back to Basics 2 Objective Evidence) to what was seen. The requirements of that document and any other extra requirements that the customer has asked for would be checked against the agreed contract document to ensure everything has been covered. The auditor will need to understand how the material to be used during the service is passed to the technician E.g Oil, Filters, etc?

How was this information passed to the technician? Do they collect their own material? Is it prepared the day before ready for the work to start the next day? What procedures or Work Instructions are in use? Do the technicians have a service schedule to work to? This is where the auditor needs to understand the process. Get the Technician to explain how it works and what documents he uses. All of this should be fully understood before the auditor can start the audit of this activity. The auditor then targets the work samples he has already chosen.

Within this process is Control of Production and service provision, **(Clause 7.5.1)** Validation of processes for service provision **(Clause 7.5.2)** Identification and traceability **(Clause 7.5.3)** if it is required Customer property **(Clause (7.5.4)**. We know this is applicable because we have the customer's car. The auditor could check if the technician knows about the responsibility for this. Ask what he would do if the car was damaged or marked during the service?

Once again all the other relevant clauses from ISO 9001 should be used as appropriate.

E.g. Document control, Records, responsibility and authority, Competence, Infrastructure, Work Environment etc etc. I will not repeat all of these as they become relevant because as already explained the ISO 9001 clauses are tools not objectives and have to be used by the auditor to judge if the processes are effective in ensuring all the contracted requirements are being covered.

Does this not highlight that to audit to see if the Management System complies with ISO 9001 clauses 4-8 is pointless? It is the skill of the auditor to utilise the clauses as appropriate to judge if the process being used is able to consistently achieve the specified requirements.

KEY 10:—From above it should be obvious that the purpose of the audit is to ensure that the Management System is adequate to ensure that each process throughout the system is able to consistently achieve and meet the required outputs.

Throughout the audit it is important that the people doing each job have the competence to carry out the tasks assigned to them. To do this they must have access to any equipment, facilities, procedures, work instructions or check list that are appropriate.

ISO 9001 4.2.3 d requires the relevant documents to be available at point of use.

It is the auditors role to check that these documents are available and controlled.

It is also important to see and make a note of what documents people are using to ascertain if they are the latest version. This is covered in clause section 4.2.3 Control of documents.

Note:—the above is applicable wherever the auditor is working.

The ability to be able to judge if a process is effective means you must follow an audit trial for the samples taken. This is why doing a process audit following an audit trail is easier and more effective than just checking items at random as you can see if the process is effective.

You use the selected sample of customer requirements to see how the information they need for this activity is passed to the technicians.

Where the items chosen are complex, very detailed and would take too long to note down, ask for an uncontrolled copy of the document e.g. a copy of a service schedule or drawing or any other relevant information. This enables cross-reference against these documents at any time during the audit so that it can be confirmed that the relevant requirements are being covered.

The auditor gathers audit evidence making notes of what works well as well as what is not effective or where defined processes are not being followed.

KEY 11: It is important to remember that selected contract requirements are being audited to see if they have been effectively dealt with and are being met. This is why the auditor must know what the contract says and take a selective sample of those requirements to see if the processes are properly controlled.

KEY 12: It is important throughout the audit to ask each auditee what procedures, instructions, check lists, forms etc they work to and note whether these are the latest version and are Controlled or Uncontrolled documents. (ISO 9001 2008 Ref 4.2.3e) The use of Uncontrolled documents at the point of use are not normally acceptable unless they are used on the day of issue.

Note:—Controlled and Uncontrolled Documents are covered in "Back to Basics Guidance Note 11 Controlled Documents.

The planning of the realisation process (7.1)

This is how the Organisation ensures that the processes and systems needed for product realisation are in place. Having chosen the Contract number/s of the car services that the auditor wishes to follow and seen the contract and what is required the auditor goes to the planning department to see how they have scheduled and passed the instructions to the shop floor. This is where any anomalies or differences to normal should have been identified and passed to the personnel carrying out the next stage. This could include the service completion date where a specific time scale has been agreed. E.g. the car has to be picked up by 13.00hrs. Has this been noted and planned into the process? It could be special delivery requirements including documents required (MoT Certificate) Standard form covering work carried out etc. The auditor is then able to verify that what has been planned can indeed ensure the product does meet specification. As stated in the ISO 9001 standard, the output of planning shall be in a form suitable for the organisations method of working.

Note:—A simple example of this is where a specific request to check the radio as it can't retain its signal has been agreed and on reviewing the planning it is seen that this has not been taken into account and passed to the vehicle technician doing the job.

Customer related processes (7.2)

This is where all the requirements of the customer are understood and agreed between both parties. Having chosen the samples the next stage is to go to the Sales or Order control department and obtain the information on the product/s chosen. It is normal to review the requirements from the customer's enquiry, any correspondence or clarification that has taken place which then leads to the agreed contract. The simplest form of contract is when the Organisation is providing a product to its own specification such as a standard service. The process then is to look at the specification identifying any special requirements or standards that are called up to ensure all the specifications are being controlled throughout the process. The more difficult type of contract is where the Customer specifies what is required, as this then brings in more interfaces over the service that is required. This could be special paint finish or non-standard interior fittings.

When auditing both above types of Contract the auditor will check National, International and Manufacturer's standards within the contract as required by ISO 9001 Sect 7.2.1c as well as any other manufacturers specifications including drawings. (If applicable) As the sample has already been chosen the standards and specification would only relate to that particular contract or service requirement.

A professional auditor will always be looking for some "Key" requirement. It may be a special material, tolerance or clearance or an unusual standard that is called up. The requirements chosen will be related to the sample product/s already chosen and a note should be made of any specific materials that need to be used along with any special requirements.

KEY 13: It is important that having identified National or International standards that are called up in the Contract that the method of ensuring they are working to the latest version is effective. Does the contract identify the applicable version? Does the system in place have access to the latest issues?

In the case of a Manufactures specific standards how the agent receives them and ensures they are the latest version

> **ANY NEW REQUIREMENTS**

7.2.2 Review of Requirements

It is possible, at any time during the service, that other issues may be identified that will need to be dealt with. This is not just applicable at the service request stage. This needs to be considered throughout the process. It is important that issues that are identified as needing attention are advised to the customer. The management system must be able to deal with this. For this process to work effectively it highlights the importance of having the information that will enable the organisation to contact the customer. Once again the process should be robust and allow for any contingency to be dealt with.

7.2.3 Customer communication

Within the customer related processes (7.2) there is a review of requirements related to the service. If during the product realisation process (work carried out) items are identified that are outside the agreed scope they would need to be dealt with. This is where the ability to manage and control any proposed changes to the agreed requirements are handled. The importance of communicating this to the customer (authorised person who may or may not be the car owner?) before taking any action could be crucial to the satisfactory completion of the service.

This is why **7.2.3 customer communication** is so important. If work is necessary then the information regarding how to contact the person who can authorise the work needs to be known. It also requires the responsible party to agree any price changes and possible change to the car pick up time etc. The need to understand how extra work can be approved should be agreed and understood by both parties right from when the initial service requirements are agreed.

Design (7.3)

Note:—In order to keep this document simple a car service has been chosen, as this does not include Design (ISO 9001 Sect 7.3)

Purchasing ISO 9001 2008 (7.4)

The requirements for the material/equipment that needs to be purchased for the sample order should be noted. It will be noticed that each section of the standard identified so far gives a rough "Check List" that can be used to decide what is required for that particular product.

KEY 14:—ISO 9001 allows exclusions from clause 7.0 Product Realisation Process where they do not affect the products ability to consistently meet the specified requirements. Other clauses apply but as appropriate to the Organisations business

It is always important to understand what drives the purchasing process. It is necessary to ensure that the contract requirements are correctly translated into the requisition. In the above case of purchasing, it is normally the requisition that defines "what is required". In the case of a main dealers car service department it may be set up on a "Call of" basis where all the parts are well controlled with specific part numbers. Prices for parts may be controlled centrally.

It does mean this could become critical where a spare part is bought in from another supplier. This is where the auditor needs to obtain the Approved Supplier List (ASL) and ensure the approval process is effective.

KEY 15:—It is important that the auditor understands the requirements of the requisition and ensures these requirements match the specification from the service contract.

If the auditor does not understand what the specification is, then the process that is being followed cannot check if the requirements of the requisition are being met.

Review what the process and activities relating to that purchasing activity are, e.g.

- What does the requisition require—does this comply with the agreed specification? 7.4
- How is the decision to purchase made? 5.5.1
- How is the specification decided? Is it adequate? 7.2.1 e.g. Special heat treated cylinder head bolts with a specified torque setting.
- Who decides what is required and do they have the authority? 5.5.1
- Who chooses the supplier and by what criteria? 7.4.1
- What is the process for bid evaluation? 7.4.1 + commercial
- How is specification advised to the supplier? 7.4.2
- Are National International standards called up? Are they the latest Version? 4.2.3
- What controls the process? 7.4
- Are there any special packing delivery requirements? 7.4.3 etc

These are a sample of issues that need to be addressed and as can be seen they refer to various clauses of ISO 9001 2008.

The starting point for the audit is to use the servicing of the cars and what needs to be changed to check if the correct material has been obtained. E.g. specific oil filter, brake pads, cambelt etc.—in the above case and for simplicity-we will take just one purchase order for a cam belt. This item is crucial to the well being of the car. Cam belts have different specifications and probably part numbers so the correct item can be fitted. Then using this sample, the auditor should identify the process taken and the controls that have been applied.

Verification of Purchased Product ISO 9001:2008 Sect 7.4.3

The next part is the receipt of the actual purchased material. It is important to check that it meets the stated requirements. The auditor should find out who does this. To what level do they inspect the item. This can take many forms and sometimes Test Certificates, Certificates of Compliance and even Quality Plans or Declarations of Conformity if it is a complete unit are required and if required, should be on the Purchase order. Once again the auditor will go through relevant purchase orders related to parts required for the sample of cars chosen. Again all these requirements should be clearly defined in the Purchase Order. Auditors should always read the Purchase Orders to ensure they are adequate and what has been called up is clear and unambiguous. The final check is probably against the Goods Inwards procedure as there may be special tests to be carried out on receipt. This may also include storage and preservation requirements. There is no point storing material incorrectly thus making it unusable. It is not unusual for personnel, in their ignorance, to open packaging and destroy the preservation that had been called up in the Purchase Order. There is sometimes a specific need to ensure that spares are used on a "First In First Out" basis (FIFO) to ensure that the oldest material is not left unused for longer than necessary. This is especially important for material that has a shelf life.

Throughout the audit process, it is vital that the samples are LINKED and from the same TRAIL. If the same trail is not followed it is not possible to comply with the scope of ISO 9001.

KEY 16:—It is, at this point, important to remind auditors how essential it is to gather audit evidence (ISO 9000 3.9.4) of what was seen.
(See Guidance Note Part 7)

Where there is no factual evidence because the auditor has only been told that something is no longer carried out, this should be noted in the report. Verbal evidence is not always reliable and further checks are often required even to confirming with the manager that this is correct. There is also Objective Evidence (See Guidance note Part 2) where the auditor writes down, in this example, the actual order number/s viewed and what was found. This would be part of the Audit Evidence (ISO 9000 3.9.4) that is used by the auditor to develop the Audit Findings (ISO 9000 3.9.5) which are then reviewed to decide what the Audit Conclusion (ISO 9000 3.9.6) will be and where necessary raise any Non Conformities (ISO 9000 3.6.2) or Observations. It should also be recognised that Professional Auditors will gather both positive and negative Audit Findings. (See Guidance note Part 6) It is unusual for auditors, when reporting that a particular process is working well, to be asked to show the evidence that supports this, however a professional auditor would be able to produce it right down to what they actually looked at.

KEY 16A Audit Evidence leads to Audit Findings that in turn leads to Audit Conclusions. This once again highlights the importance of a common understanding being achieved by using ISO 9000 definitions.

KEY 17:—Always follow the chosen Audit Trail as it is too easy for auditors to take samples at different stages of the process that are not related or linked to the sample/s chosen. This only allows the auditor to be able to check if a document is filled in correctly, missing out on being able to verify that the process is actually working.

During the above audit process the procedures, forms, check lists etc are all reviewed and checked to ensure the process is managed and controlled effectively.

KEY 18:—The importance of starting the service with the correct spares for the parts being changed is paramount as using the wrong material would ensure the service did not meet specification. It should be noted any change in material must have formal approval.

Note:—Although not relevant to this example but important to auditing in general the use of the so called 'better' grade of material without design change justification and approval is never acceptable.

Customer property ISO 9001:2008 Sect 7.5.4

Where a Customer provides something that is in the Organisation's control, either to be put into the product or provided so that the work may take place, the requirements for looking after and controlling that material applies. This requirement is basic common sense and in many cases it may not be applicable. (Exemption would be identified in the Quality manual) In this case the vehicle is customer property and has to be looked after while the work is carried out as such the vehicle is a deliverable all be it a serviced deliverable.

Preservation of product ISO 9001:2008 Sect 7.5.5

The same goes for Preservation of the product. Having now ensured that all the correct material needed to carry out the service is acceptable it is the time to get into the actual service itself. It is important that throughout the process of carrying out the service the material to be used is kept in good condition. Some items may be stock items and called off as required. How these items are stored can impact on the ability to utilise the material when it is needed. This preservation is applicable right through out the service and delivery process.

Production and Service Provision ISO 9001 Sect 7.5

For this area Scheduled Drawings (Design approved drawings) and working drawings (Sometimes called related drawings) need to be examined (Refer 7.5.1). This together with any other information on the product should be noted as should any special requirements. Once again the Auditor would restrict what is viewed to the relevant drawings, check list etc for the sample already chosen. The control of the documents can often be critical. It is important to identify the "latest version" of all relevant drawings, check lists, standard forms etc and then take samples of any documents that are important to the Audit Trail being followed. They may have special clearances, tolerances, torque settings, testing processes etc.

During the audit process drawings and other working documents will be examined to ensure the process is being adhered to and that versions on the shop floor are in fact the latest version.

If this is not understood and checked then the audit is not professional. There is often a "Route Card" or "Check List" that goes with the order or a batch. The "Route Card" or "Check List" shows what should happen even include the required clearances etc that may be required and these are signed off or initialled to show it has been done. It is this verification throughout the process that demonstrates that the processes have been carried out, checked and signed off. This Route Card or Check List can also become a record for the service of the vehicle. Once again working Procedures, Check Lists and Forms all have to be examined to ensure the process is working effectively. The audit trail will lead the auditor to the correct documents. It is not unusual for someone to indicate they cannot locate that signed checklist for the sample order and offer one for a different order. This of course is not acceptable as it is not relevant to the audit trail being followed. These signed off "Check lists" are nearly always records that require retention. Again the retention time and disposal time etc should be checked for that document (ISO 9001 Ref 4.2.4). The Auditor should understand what documents are kept as records and how long they are retained.

Note:—It is not the intention of this document to go through each individual process for all parts that make up the order, however the auditor will take samples and follow those chosen samples through to ensure they are controlled effectively.

KEY 19 Auditing of the process would entail physically reviewing what is taking place by sampling specific items and witnessing any tolerances required such as "Torque settings" for head tightening, "Cam belt tensioning settings". Auditing is not just a paper exercise.

Control of Monitoring and Measuring Equipment ISO 9001:2008 Ref 7.6

During the servicing of the car and when it is complete, the vehicle may need testing or calibrating etc. again it is important to check that this is carried out correctly. There may have been different monitoring and measuring devices identified throughout the servicing of the car and their relevant identification number should have been noted together with the date for next calibration. There are often electronic testing facilities that analyse the performance of the vehicle and are able to identify problems before they become obvious to the technician or the car owner. This type of equipment also has to be proven to be accurate to the relevant standards. This equipment should be identified together with any equipment used in final testing as these items should be checked to ensure they are in calibration and the time between each calibration is realistic. Check the records of the results of calibration to ensure all is in control (ISO 9001 7.6).

The purpose of calibration is to ensure that monitoring and measuring equipment is accurate. To this end it is important to ensure that calibration is carried out in a manner that ensures it is accurate and any supplier the organisation uses to provide this service (Contractor) must be able to demonstrate that they are competent and can trace the accuracy back to National/International standards. They should also be on the approved supplier list and their competence in this matter should be clearly defined and registered within the system. On one particular audit carried out by the author the calibrated equipment only had the date of the last calibration. This is not helpful as personnel using the equipment should be able to see before they use the equipment if the instrument is still in calibration. This requires the calibration due date to be defined on the instrument.

> **COMPLETE SERVICE**

Preservation of Product ISO 9001:2008 Ref 7.5.5

The final part of the audit process is to ensure the product is delivered to the customer in good condition. Preservation of the vehicle throughout the service is also covered within this section.

Once again, the process for ensuring the service is complete is normally the receipt of the documents covering what was carried out during the service. It is the auditor's job to verify that the process in place is suitable and the release of the vehicle is controlled and adequate?

> **SERVICE REPORT**

Are there any documents that have to be given to the customer? How and who carries this out? Is there a need to provide any advice or instructions following the service. Are their any advisory warnings regarding future maintenance or repair requirements? There may also be a need to provide an MOT certificate or service record document showing what work was carried out. All of this should have been defined in the contract with the customer or required in the organisations own system.

It is always the responsibility of the Organisation to ensure the vehicle is kept in good condition and it may include cleaning the vehicle before being picked up or delivered to the Customer's location.

KEY 20:—*Auditing of a process must follow an audit trail or it is impossible to verify that requirements are being met.*

> **ADVISE CUSTOMER OF WORK DONE AND RELEASE VEHICLE**

This is an important part of the process. It is where all the work carried out will be explained. If there was any damage this will also be advised to the customer. If the car has been cleaned this will also be mentioned. There is normally where the cost of the service is explained and cross-referenced against the work carried out. It is where any extra work is also explained and this would normally have been agreed with the customer before it was carried out. The paper work would be completed with any certificates e.g. MOT provided. This will be checked against the original agreed service requirements. If there is any guidance suggestion regarding how the car should be driven for a period of time such as bed brake shoes in for the next 100 miles etc then the vehicle owner would also be advised. Finally the payment would be made and the keys returned to the owner. Finishing with advising the owner where the car is located.

It is essential that the auditor take's the time to understand what is required from the process. This means understanding what is "specified" (Input v Output) regarding any process they may be asked to audit. Auditors who do not know what the output from any process should be are not carrying out an effective audit.

> **CUSTOMER COMPLAINTS**

Any complaints would be dealt with at this point or if a problem arises after the car has been driven. Again this would need to be registered and the auditor would look to see what complaints have been made and how the organisation deals with them. It may be registered as a Non conformity (8.3). This covers taking action to eliminate the nonconformity (Known as Correction). If any correction has been taken then it would need to be re verified to demonstrate that the non-conformity has been removed. It is the auditors role to ensure they are not only corrected but proper corrective action has taken place by getting back to the "Root Cause" of the problem in order to prevent it happening again. There is a misunderstanding about Corrective Action and the term CAPA (Corrective Action and Preventative Action). This acronym has unfortunately established itself within quality circles as an acceptable term. Please be aware that preventive action is **NOT** the action taken during corrective action. **Preventive Action has a specific role and if something has already gone wrong and needs correcting then this is not preventative action**. I ask all quality professionals to read ISO 9001 clauses 8.5.2 and 8.5.3. as they are quite clear.

KEY 21 The term "CAPA" should NOT be used to link the terms Corrective Action (CA) and Preventative Action (PA) as they are not related when being used in ISO 9001.

It is not the intention within this book to cover everything that an auditor needs to do. As explained at the beginning it is to explain the importance of doing a process audit following an audit trail. Doing audits in this manner actually makes auditing more effective and believe it or not simpler. This is because you restrict the audit to just the sample of contracts that you have selected.

It is hoped that the example illustrated demonstrates how effective an audit can be. There are too many examples of audits auditing the clauses of the specified standard not even looking at what the process is supposed to achieve.

SIMPLE Process Audit Trail

As can be seen so far the samples taken give some idea of what Process Audits following an Audit Trail are about. Lets imagine that one of the vehicles in your sample was having a Head gasket changed. This required new bolts to be used and the bolts were a specific alloy steel that required heat treatment. To make this clearer these bolts have been selected by you as your sample from the product realisation process. They will be taken and viewed from a process flow perspective. The sample chosen as mentioned is a bolt as most people know what a bolt is. These bolts were seen to be Special Hardened Bolts with Material Certificates and a special torque setting. It is assumed for this exercise that all this information came from one drawing.

The relevant Procedures and Work Instructions Check Lists etc used during each process should be checked to see if the process is being followed. The version of each document needs to be noted and checked to see if it is the latest version.

Let the specification be Metric 12mm High Tensile Bolts partially threaded steel grade 10.9 super fine threads with a pitch of 1.25 requiring a Material Certificate.

a) The auditor would note the drawing number and the issue number. Is this drawing the latest version? (4.2.3) This needs to be checked. Is it approved?
b) The next stage would be to check the Requisition for the product specification. Does this contain the full description of the bolt and any special requirements. Who develops this and who has the responsibility and authority, are they competent? (The competence, responsibility and authority will be relevant throughout each step of the process). The requirement may even specify a particular manufacture or supplier that must be used.
c) Has the Purchase order taken into account all the requirements defined in the requisition? Has it defined any specific requirements e.g. Material Certificate.
d) How are the bolts checked on receipt are they traceable back to the purchase order? Is there a check on the thread form and bolt size? (Thread Gauging)
e) Has the Material certificate been provided, how is this accepted? How do they know it has been heat-treated? Does the procedure explain what checks are made and by whom. This is where other Audits (Supplier/Vendor) were valuable as the full report was available as was historical information on

past performance. In some instances "A" rated suppliers needed no goods inwards inspection or checks. Goods were accepted on receipt and spares from the car manufacturer may be in this category. What is the Organisations control over how these items are accepted? What controls goods inwards inspection? Are there relevant Procedures/Work Instructions?

f) How are the bolts stored and accessed for this particular order? Are the Bolts stock items? How do the stored bolts and the material certificates retain their trace ability?

g) During the manufacturing and assembly how are the bolts tightened to the specified torque setting. How is the Torque Wrench calibrated and status identified.

h) How, if required, is the Material Certificate for the bolts supplied to the Customer and how can this be traced back to the specific bolts used in that contract?

The detail of the above will vary dependent on the criticality of the bolt and whether the part is directly from the manufacturer or from another supplier. That is why confidence in the ability of any supplier to meet the specified requirements is critical. The author has seen bolts and even critical shafts machined out of the correct material but without any heat treatment. These items actually failed when put in service. Professional auditing can identify this.

KEY 22:—*It is important to follow the same item throughout the activity to verify that the process is controlled and could ensure that the full specification was achieved each time.*

As can be seen this is the audit trail of a bolt, just one of the items identified for following during the audit. The objective is to ensure it meets the specified requirements. These bolts could be critical as illustrated by the aeroplane that had the cockpit screen blow out when coming into land. This was due to incorrect bolts being fitted. Thankfully everyone survived the incident and it is believed that no one was seriously injured. Auditors should be looking to ensure that the processes being used for each of the sampled items are not only effective but are in control. It does of course depend on the critical nature of any item and the Organisation should have addressed this.

General Summary

The Audit Trail approach to auditing should be applied to any Organisation as long as it is known what activity is carried out. It is always important for the auditor to know what the Organisation has agreed to do and to what specification. The need to understand what each process is required to achieve allows the auditor, following an audit Trail, to ensure that each requirement can be met.

There is a common misconception that the above is a technical audit. This is incorrect as the purpose of an audit is to ascertain if the management system can consistently meet the specified requirements. You cannot carry out an audit without knowing what the output is supposed to be. A technical audit is where you ascertain if the product or service can actually achieve the intended purpose of the product or service. The BSI Kitemark is a method of ensuring that the product itself can meet its intended purpose.

An ISO 9001 Quality Audit is to see if the quality management system is capable of consistently meeting the specified requirements for the product or service. This cannot be done if you do not know what the output is supposed to be. (ISO 9001 Scope refers)

KEY 23
A quality audit does not indicate that the product itself is suitable for what it will be used for just that the organisation can consistently make the product to the agreed specified requirements.

A recent discussion on this indicated that many senior quality professionals believe that if the ISO 9001 system is **not** used effectively then it is the organisations responsibility. ISO 9001 certification is just to indicate they have a system. What a poor service we provide if that is all ISO 9001 Certification means because it does not achieve the purpose of ISO 9001. I again ask readers to look at the scope of ISO

9001 as it clearly states that it specifies the requirements for a quality management system where an organisation needs to demonstrate its ability to consistently provide product that meets customer and applicable statutory and regulatory requirements. If you do not check that the process in use is effective what is the point of the audit? The "Tick Box" approach against the clause 4-8 is disgraceful and cannot possibly meet the intention and scope of ISO 9001.

This document now majors on service, all be it a car service which some may find a little technical, however the basic principle of following an Audit Trail applies to all audits. There is a belief that it is only possible to audit if there are procedures. This is not true as there is NO specific statement in ISO 9001, or in real life, that states you always need procedures, in fact the ISO 9001 versions from 2000 removed the need to have many procedures and now only six clauses have a stated mandatory requirement to have a procedure. ISO 9001 4.2.1d then goes on to indicate that the system should only include documents determined by the Organisation to be necessary to ensure effective planning, operation and control. The point being made is the Organisation decides what is needed in the way of a documented Management System.

KEY 24 Auditors should have some knowledge and competence in the product or service being carried out. This then enables them to accept that procedures and work instructions etc may not be necessary where competent personnel are being used.

This can lead to an Organisation where no formal documented system exists for a particular activity yet the process could still be audited. The approach to use is to have a "Walk Through" with someone explaining what takes place. The auditor will make notes or draw a simple flow chart whilst going through the process. The auditor is then able to choose a few examples and follow the process through to see how effective it is. If different personnel are involved in the same process the auditor would sample the work of a number of personnel. If the Auditees can demonstrate, because of their competence and training, that they can consistently follow the stated process and the output can be relied upon then this would be acceptable.

A simple example of a process is making tea. Is there a procedure needed? Is it possible to train personnel to make tea in a consistent acceptable manner? Then of course there is an example of the Japanese Tea ceremony that can take many years of training. Is a procedure needed? The Organisation itself decides.

Process of tea Making

Let us look at an Organisation that provides refreshment such as tea.

TEA

Lets imagine we are auditing this Tea House do they need to have a procedure for the person providing the tea?

It may not be necessary to have anything however they would have to ensure the person was competent. ISO 9000:2005 "Competence" is the demonstrated ability to apply knowledge and skills. The new ISO 19011:2011 definition for "Competence" sates it is the ability to apply knowledge and skills to achieve intended results. The late version does not have to have "Demonstrated ability". Luckily at present ISO 9001 states in clause 2 Normative references that ISO 9000:2005 is indispensable for the application of ISO 9001 and that only the dated version is applicable so ISO 9000:2005 is relevant at present.

Please see authors other book "ISO 9000 Family of Standards" where even the term "Auditor" has been redefined in ISO 19011:2011 in what the author believes is an inappropriate manner.

It is up to the Organisation to decide what is necessary. How do you ensure someone is competent? You can of course train them and then see if they can **demonstrate** they are competent. Who decides what is the correct way to make tea? How is that person judged to be competent? What is the correct way to make tea? Is there only one way?

As you can see this has already highlighted many questions.

Lets look at one method the method used by my parents.
What do you need to make tea?

- Tea itself, Water, Kettle, Teapot (China glazed), Cup (China), Saucer (China) Milk, Sugar, Tray, Tea Spoon

Process. (1950's)

1. Put water in the kettle and boil it
2. Poor some boiling water in the Teapot and swirl it round to heat the teapot.
3. Put the correct quantity of tea in the heated teapot. (One teaspoon per person plus one more for the pot)
4. Re boil the kettle and add enough water to the teapot for one more cup than the people requiring tea and stir.
5. Put tea cosy over teapot to keep tea warm and allow it to "Draw".
6. Allow to stand for one to two minutes (varies with type of tea used)
7. Put teapot, milk, sugar, teaspoons, cups and saucers on the tray.
8. Deliver to customers
9. Pour tea into teacups then top up the tea pot with enough boiling water for a second cup each. Again stir and replace tea cosy.

Note Some people put the tea in first then add the sugar and milk others put the milk in first then add the tea.

10. Pour second cup of tea as required.
11. Use tray to collect the used utensils and return for washing up.

Process. (after 1970's)

1. Put water in the kettle and boil it
2. Put one tea bag for each person in the teapot (or cup if teapot not used)
3. Pour boiling water on the teabag in the cup or teapot.

4. Stir and allow to stand for one minute (varies with type of tea used)
5. Put, milk, sugar, teaspoons, cups and saucers on the tray.
6. Deliver to customers

Note 1 Some people put the tea in first then add the sugar and milk others put the milk in first then add the tea.

Note 2 Sometimes the boiling water is put in a separate pot. The problem with this is the water is no longer boiling when it is poured onto the tea in the teapot/cup.

7. Use tray to collect the used utensils and return for washing up.

Is this progress? It is quicker and easier. Does it improve the quality of the tea? Which version makes the best cup of tea?

Process. (after 1990's)

American and Hotel tea

1. Put one tea bag in the cup
2. Provide hot water (Not boiling)
3. Put your own hot water in cup with tea bag in it
4. Stir and allow to stand (varies with type of tea used)
5. Put, milk, sugar, teaspoons, on your self service tray.
6. Obtain your own small carton of milk.

The KEY point of raising this is I am trying to make people understand that the ISO 9001 auditing is NOT about whether the product is a good product but can the organisation consistently make the product to the required specification? ISO 9004 is the standard for assessing if the product is what the customer wants as it is able to address the broader issue of quality to ensure the sustained success of an organisation.

ISO 9001 Audit Trail

YOU CANNOT MAKE TEA UNLESS YOU USE BOILING WATER.
BECAUSE IT DOES NOT TASTE RIGHT.

This may be true, however if the organisation has decided this is how they make tea then the auditor just confirms they can consistently meet their specified requirements.

I guess auditing is the same because you will have understood by now you can't audit unless you use boiling water. I mean do a process audit following an audit trail

PLEASE NOTE THIS IS A LIGHT HEARTED APPROACH TO A QUALITY PROCESS

Auditors activities

If there is no procedure or work instruction ask the Organisation to show you what happens. A good way is to walk through the process. Make notes on the process. There may be a checklist for taking the order. It may have the till with the individual items having a specific key to press for that item. The auditor should have seen this when walking through the process.

You know what takes place and you are now in a position to start your audit.

YOU CAN ONLY AUDIT SOMETHING IF YOU KNOW WHAT THE OUTCOME SHOULD BE. ANY OTHER METHOD IS POINTLESS

The point of this summary is to explain the standard can be used for any activity as it allows the auditor to dip into the ISO 9001 clauses to ascertain if the process is properly controlled. It is not up to the auditor to say the Organisation needs a procedure, even if during the audit a process was found to be ineffective it would be the Organisation that would have to decide how to tackle this. The auditor should know the ISO 9001 standard and its clauses and have a good understanding of the process being audited. The auditor then dips into the "Tool Box" of clauses to see if the process is able to consistently meet the specified requirements. A successful audit is dependent upon the competence and ability of the auditor to make it professional and beneficial.

KEY 25:—It is not the Audit Trail of the procedure that is followed but the Audit Trail of the process.

I have been told that using an audit trail is not always necessary when carrying out an audit. When asked what would be audited without following an audit trail I was advised when auditing the documented system. Unfortunately you do not audit the documented system.

This stems from what was called the Document Review where an organisation's Quality Manual is examined to see if it has recognized, and addressed all the requirements of ISO 9001 in principle. This "desktop" stage 1 audit is a specific training element from a Lead Auditor Course. It should be recognised that the Quality Manual is just a stated intent nothing more. It is a commitment explaining "WHAT" an Organisation does. It does not have to cover Why, When, How, Where and Who. The true situation is only revealed, at the levels below the Quality Manual, when a professional **process audit** is carried out to ascertain if the processes that have been put in place can consistently achieve the specified requirements.

How can an auditor ascertain if the process is able to consistently meet the specified requirements if they do not know what the specification for the product is?

I was also told you don't follow an audit trail when auditing the Management review. I pointed out that you would sample the last two or three management reviews to ascertain if the actions from the earlier meetings had been completed and closed in an effective manner. This is following an audit trail. You identify what was agreed to be carried out (Action) then verify that it has been done in a manner that ensures the problem does not recur.

Some time ago I had a letter published about hospital audits. I believe that in many cases, like some ISO audits, the auditor is only being asked to audit to see if the clauses of the relevant standard are covered. It is this failure to audit to see if the process is effective that undermines audits and costs organisation a lot of money with little return. This is highlighted when the hospital audit indicates that the management system is good yet the actual service being provided is very poor. It again demonstrates that auditing to see if clauses of the standard are covered in the management system tells you nothing about how effective the process is. This actually occurred when hospitals received good audit ratings yet the service to the customer was abysmal. The type of auditing I am talking about would improve the service to both the organisation itself and the customers of that organisation. To do this type of audit you must have an understanding and knowledge of the organisations business activities. This type of audit requires auditor competence and needs the auditor to understand what the outcome of any process should be. The current "Tick Box" auditing of procedures achieves little.

What is disappointing is that so many people do not follow any trail at all. They just check if the organisation has done what the procedure says using any evidence that happens to be around at the time. There is often no link between one document seen and any other so you can only verify that the piece of paper has been filled in correctly not that the process is working effectively. I have to say that it is not the auditors fault because in many cases that is what they have been taught. The purpose of this document and the book on the "ISO 9000 Family of Standards" is to improve quality training by understanding the purpose of the ISO 9000 Family of Standards and improving the standard of auditing.

KEY 26:—In the closing meeting the Organisation would be advised that the audit was by sampling and that because nothing had been identified to be wrong it did not mean that everything was correct.

8.0 Concerns

As can be seen this document attempts to identify some relevant clauses in ISO 9001 as they are used within a **Process Audit** following an **Audit Trail**.

Note:—Remember it is not possible to audit everything that goes into a product or Service that is why "Selective Sampling" is so important.

8.1 Tick List Approach

This "Tick" list approach without understanding the requirement of the process is a complete and utter waste of time. It seems it is more important to report that one element of the standard is not covered in the management system than whether the product/service meets the specified requirement. If an element is missing its "Tick" it is considered to be a significant issue without considering how important it is to the Product/Service being provided.

This again highlights how far the auditing activity has moved away from the original intention of ensuring that the Organisation needs to demonstrate its ability to consistently provide product that meets customer and applicable statutory and regulatory requirements.

Remember ISO 9001 is a tool and no one needs to use every tool in the toolbox to ensure that an Organisation does have a management system that meets the specified requirements. This is where the skill of the auditor comes in when they choose the relevant clauses.

KEY 27:—Some auditors spend more time ensuring each element of the ISO 9001 Standard has a "Tick" against it than ensuring the system is effective.

8.2 Improvement Opportunity

The author has raised the concern over what has happened to ISO 9001 Certification and how through poor understanding of what is required the credibility of ISO Certification is very low. This document following on from the two articles on Audit Trail written in IRCA Inform and ISO 9001 Auditing Practices Groups website is the start of an **improvement project**. It is recognised that it will take 3 to 5 years to achieve credibility, however to sit back and do nothing should not be an option.

An improvement Project has been proposed in the authors new book "ISO 9000 Family of Standards" and the first 5 pages of this document is attached as Appendix D. It has also been sent to the International Accreditition Forum (IAF) because unless all accreditation bodies can agree on the proposed 5 year improvement plan nothing will happen. If any Organisation, or individual, wishes to become part of the solution rather than part of the problem please contact the author **info@pdqms.co.uk**. Or **daveseear@btinternet.com**

The auditing as described follows the Primary process and majors on Product realisation (Section 7) and it should be recognised it does not cover every clause within ISO 9001 2008 separately as everything outside Section 7 supports the primary process and can be considered as a support to that process.

Auditors must understand the Documentation requirements and how the documented system is issued and controlled (4.2.3) and what records (4.2.4) are kept.

This means at every stage of the audit it is important to ask the auditee what procedures, work instructions, forms etc they work with. It is also important to understand if these documents are controlled documents. The difference between controlled and uncontrolled documents can and does cause considerable problems.

(See Guidance Note Part 11 Controlled Documents)

ISO 9001 section 5 covers management responsibility and in particular 5.5 Responsibility, authority and communication. This covers who performs what activity and with what authority. For the purposes of this document the requirements for management review 5.6 has been ignored. In fact some managers think the management review is a Quality System requirement and nothing to do with the Product or Service that is provided. The Quality Management System is the organisations management system used to manage the Product or Service provision. It is important that Management recognise that the QMS and the Management Review should cover all aspects of managing the production of the Product/Service.

The statement that Management Review takes place once a year is a nonsense and has been perpetuated by auditors accepting this. When the auditor asks the Organisation how often they carry out management reviews it is normally at least quarterly or even more frequently. It is just that Quality is seen as something separate when it should be a review of their actual management system.

The section on resource management, ISO 9001 section 6 is also relevant throughout the whole organisation. It is not unusual to see that some Organisations still audit Training as a separate entity. This will tell the auditor nothing except someone has kept the paperwork up to date. Does it really show they are using competent personnel in all the relevant roles? This is where the list of all personnel seen during the audit can be used to see if the training system records confirmed that personnel were competent in the work they were seen to be doing. That is why the visit to the training department is later in the Audit Plan.

Section 8 is only addressed with Monitoring and measuring of processes but it is important to ensure the Organisation improves and Internal Audit is a "Key" element of this. The techniques used in this document are applicable to Internal Audits.

As stated at the beginning of this document only a small number of areas have been covered as an example of what Process Audit following an Audit Trail is all about.

KEY 28:—Professional Auditing is NOT about seeing if the management system complies with ISO 9001 clause 4-8 but seeing that the system used within that Organisation is capable of consistently achieving the intended outcome.

This can only be done by following an Audit Trail.

NOTE:—It should be born in mind that this document is a simplistic approach to explain what an Audit Trail is about. It is the skill of the auditor that decides which trail needs to be followed and for how long. This can only be done once the auditor has understood what the product or service is and what within that process needs to be chosen to demonstrate that this is effective.

ALWAYS REMEMBER

1.0 The system should work for you not you work for the system

2.0 ISO 9001 is to enable organisations to demonstrate that they can consistently meet the customer and applicable statutory and regulatory requirements.

3.0 ISO 9004 is used to pick up the remaining management requirements to enable them to manage for the sustained success of an organisation.

4.0 If Organisations, Certification Bodies and Auditors did not try to lever the ISO 9004 requirements into ISO 9001 life would be simpler.

5.0 ISO 9001 introduction clause 0.4 "Compatibility with other management systems" indicates that environment, safety and risk are not applicable. Trying to add other management requirements into ISO 9001 should not be countenanced as it has a restrictive role that excludes many other management systems.

6.0 If we, as quality professionals ask organization to improve shouldn't we accept that maybe we should look at ways of improving the benefits from an ISO 9001 audit?

9.0 Summary of Simple Audit Flow

1. Have a walk around the Organisation. Get to understand the layout and see what is taking place at that time. Identify some Contracts/Orders that are actually going through. (Note Contract will be used for customer orders)
2. Check the planning for the sampled products and identify how this is handled.
3. Visit the sales department and see what the final agreement was between the Organisation and the Customer for the chosen sampled contracts. Review any modifications and changes that may have been made and ensure that these changes are controlled and agreement obtained between both parties.
4. Review the chosen contracts in detail identifying any specific requirements regarding material to be used, standards and or drawings to be used and any special requirements. Identify the latest issue of all documents. Note the number and issue status of relevant documents such as drawings, material specification against International standards and any odd or special requirements.
5. Find out how the contract requirements are identified and input into the requisition for the material. Go through how this material is purchased and verify that the process does indeed ensure that the purchase order does include all the requirements including Material Certificates, Test Certificates etc that may be necessary to ensure the material ordered is in fact correct.
6. Cover how the goods received are checked to ensure what was ordered was in fact what was delivered. Ensure material received is properly looked after in the stores and how the issue of material to the stores is controlled with reference to relevant material certificates.
7. Identify what instructions and documents control the manufacture or service of the chosen product/service. Go through the process ensuring that the process is well controlled and all the called up requirements are adhered to. Identify signed off check lists, travellers, Route cards etc and any other outputs required e.g. Test Results to see they are complete and

the correct authorised persons have signed off the relevant documents.

8. Identify any monitoring and Measuring devices and ensure they are identified with the next due date for calibration. Use the sample taken to verify the records for this activity are properly controlled and correct.

9. Identify how the finished product is approved for release. Who has the authority and what checks and controls apply. It is important to identify what documents need to be sent with the product. Items such as Material Certificates, Test Reports, Operating Instructions, Certificates of Compliance (C of C) and even Declarations of Conformity (D of C). These are just a few of the possible requirements that may be required.

Remember that the objective is to verify that the Management System is capable of ensuring that all the Customer Contracts/Purchase Orders can consistently meet the specified requirements. The above concentrates on the Primary Process and there is of course all the Secondary Processes that support this that needs to be verified throughout the audit.

REMEMBER ISO 9001 2008 IS A TOOL NOT AN OBJECTIVE

To do this the auditor needs to follow the Product realisation process (Sect 7) using the other sections of ISO 9001 to verify that the supporting requirements are adequate to achieve this.

It is this ability to cross-reference the needs of the process against how the sample chosen is controlled and managed that is Key to a Professional Audit.

10.0 Conclusion

10.1 ISO 9001 is a TOOL not an OBJECTIVE

10.2 ISO 9001 Certification is to give Purchasers confidence in the certified Organisations ability to consistently meet the specified requirements.

10.3 Audits should NOT be a "Tick List" approach to see if the Organisations Management System complies with ISO 9001 clauses 4-8. This approach will, by itself, give little or no confidence in the Organisations ability to meet the specified requirements.

10.4 All Audits should be PROCESS AUDITS following an AUDIT TRAIL.

10.5 By following an audit trail the audit should, by auditing a specific customer order/contract, be able to verify that the Organisations Management System is capable of consistently controlling the process thereby ensuring products/services meet the specified requirements.

10.6 Statutory and Regulatory requirements called up in ISO 9001 are only those that relate to the requirements of the product or service being audited.

10.7 Failure to carry out a Process Audit following an Audit Trail is the single most important reason why audits are not effective.

10.8 Where auditors only audit the procedural system, not the process and its intended outcome, it could well show that nothing is wrong. This approach gives no confidence in the processes ability to meet specified requirements

10.9 Audits should add value and be beneficial

10.10 Internal Audits only carried out because the ISO 9001 standard says so without adding value are a waste of time and pointless.

10.11 Professional audits are beneficial to an Organisation as they either confirm that the process is effective or, if not, allows action to be taken to correct the weaknesses highlighted.

10.12 Professional Auditing is NOT about seeing if the management system complies with ISO 9001 but seeing that the system used within that Organisation is capable of consistently meeting the specified contract requirements.

GENERAL COMMENT

It is worth noting that all auditing would benefit from understanding what the requirements are whether it is Environment, Health and Safety, or any other auditing activity as there are too many auditors, auditing to see if the Relevant Standard is being followed and not auditing to see if processes being used are appropriate and able to achieve the intended outcome.

All types of audit would benefit from verifying that each Process is effective. This can only be verified by following an AUDIT TRAIL.

11.0 Back to Basics Guidance Documents

The "Back to Basics" documents were developed over many years of practical experience in order to assist students on the IRCA Auditor Courses. They covered some of the most misunderstood areas of the auditing activities.

WARNING

The documents that follow are not in any special order and do not always have approved formal definitions where they do they are identified. It should be recognised that in running training courses it is important to explain how each of the terms below may be used.

Each of these "Back to Basics" documents are written as "Stand Alone" documents so there is some repetition within these documents.

As shown in the case of "Audit Trail" there is no definition and that is why it is only a suggested definition. Also D of C and C of C have different interpretation but are becoming used more often and may need a common ISO definition as even C of C has different wording depending on who is using it.

GUIDANCE DOCUMENTS

1. Audit Trail
2. Objective Evidence
3. Specification
4. Audit Criteria
5. Random Sample
6. Audit Findings
7. Audit Evidence
8. Competence
9. Declaration Of Conformity (D of C)
10. Certificates of Compliance (C of C)
11. Controlled Documents
12. Certification

It is recognised that not all personnel may accept all the comments in each Guidance Note but hopefully it may start a discussion that will resolve any issue of concern.
e.g. Audit Trail
The author would be pleased to receive any constructive comments both positive and negative in order to improve these guidance notes.

Part 1 Audit Trail

Audit trail is one of the most important aspects of Auditing. If an audit trail is not followed then most that can be checked is whether the individual documents looked at are correctly filled in.

Dictionary Definitions

Audit
An Examination by qualified persons of, accounts of a business, public office or **an undertaking.**

Normally related to Financial Activities but latterly used by Quality Practioner's to assess the ability of an Organisation to comply with specified requirements.

Trail
Part drawn behind or in the wake of a thing
Track left by thing that has been moved or been drawn over a surface.
Track, scent or **beaten path.**
If the above are linked together we have:—

Audit Trail

**An examination, by a qualified person, of an activity
Following the path that has been left by the process.**

So what does this mean?
Take a simple purchasing activity
How is the decision to purchase made? Who decides what is required and do they have the authority? How is this advised to the supplier? Who chooses the supplier and by what criteria? How is the specification decided? Is it adequate?

- It is essential that a sample is chosen (This is the starting point)
- Then use the sample/s to identify the process taken such as:—

- o What drove the process e.g. what controls the process, how are decisions made.
- o Who has the authority
- o Who decides quantities
- o Who decides specification
- o How is specification controlled

The most important thing is to ensure that the samples are LINKED that they are from the same TRAIL.

If the Auditor is following the trail of a HORSE there is no point ending up behind a DONKEY.

Note:—this was the first and the original document issued in 2006 after ISO 9000 2005 had been issued

Part 2 Objective Evidence

This is, together with "Audit Trail", one of the most important aspects for an Auditor to understand if they are to do professional audits. From past experience it is not always easily understood.

ISO 9000: 2005 section **3.8.1 Objective Evidence** is data supporting the existence or verity (Truth) of something.
Why is it important?
If there is Objective Evidence there can be No Dispute over the findings.

What is "Objective Evidence"

First look at "**Audit Findings**". **Section 3.9.5** of ISO 9000: 2000 defines
Audit Findings as:—
results of the evaluation of the collected **Audit Evidence (3.9.4)** against the **Audit Criteria (3.9.3).**

Audit evidence can be:—

1) Factual statements such as:—
- form SF 203 is no longer used.
2) Visual evidence such as:—
- the 12mm washers were kept in the storage shelf for the 25 mm washers.
3) Documented Evidence such as:—
- Five Purchase Orders were reviewed No's 230, 252, 276, 301 and 303 and two purchase orders No's 301 and 303 were not signed by the senior Buyer as required by Procedure QP 27 paragraph 16.2.

The factual statement 1) above, where something is no longer used, cannot be verified by Objective Evidence because actual evidence doesn't exist.

Visual evidence 2) can be **Objective Evidence** if in the example above the location of the washers e.g. Bin Number 21 should contain the 12mm washers yet the 12mm washers were in bin Number 29 which should, according to the stores log sheet, contain the 25mmm washers.

Note:—The Auditee would need to obtain the Auditee or Guides agreement with this finding.

Documented evidence may be **Objective Evidence** if the specific items seen are identified and documented within the findings. It should be noted that the two purchase orders mentioned in 3) above that are not signed by the Senior Buyer e.g. P.O. 301 and 303 are, when written in the Non Conformity, objective evidence.

This may sound a little confusing but put **Objective Evidence** in the simplest form

Objective Evidence is where **"IF CHALLENGED"** the Auditor can easily go back to the specific item looked at because it is identified in the report and the Non Conformity.

If it is not possible to go back to the specific item of concern it would NOT be "OBJECTIVE EVIDENCE".
e.g. Non Conformity

"Procedure QP 27 Rev 4 Para 16.2 requires all Purchase Orders to be signed by the Senior Buyer. Two of the five purchase orders seen were not signed by the senior buyer".

Looks good? Wrong!! This non-conformity has no Objective evidence because it has not included the P.O. Numbers 301 and 303.

Part 3 Specification

The term **"Specification"** (3.7.3) is defined in ISO 9000 2005 as:—
Document stating requirements.

It is impossible to carry out a Professional Audit if the auditor has not looked at the **document stating the requirements** for any process that may be audited.

Lets also look at **Audit (3.9.1)**
Systematic, independent and documented process for obtaining audit evidence and evaluating it objectively to determine the extent to which audit criteria are fulfilled.

We will come to **audit criteria** later in the guidance documents however one audit criteria for ISO 9001 audits is, of course, the ISO 9001 2008 standard itself. There are people who believe they are there to Audit to see if "the system complies with ISO 9001 2008!!"

However they forget then to look at the standard itself that clearly states within the Scope:—

1.1 General section

This International Standard specifies requirements for a quality management system where an organisation:—

> **needs to demonstrate its ability to consistently provide a product that meets customer and applicable regulatory requirements.**

The purpose of the audit is to see if the Management System is able to control the process in a manner that can ensure the product or service can consistently be met. The method of doing this is by judging the process used against the clauses within the ISO 9001 standard to verify that the system can achieve this.

Which then leads us back to **specification.**

The document stating requirements is usually the Purchase order or contract received from their customer. It is sometimes difficult for new auditors to understand that the term purchase order is used both for Customers Purchase Orders and the Organisation own Purchase Orders used to obtain material from their suppliers. For simplicity, in this article, **we will refer to customer requirements as the "Contract"**.

The simplest form of contract is when the Organisation is making a product to its own specification. The process then is to look at the specification identifying any special requirements or standards that are called up and going through Section 7 of ISO 9001 2008 (Product Realisation) to ensure all the specifications are being controlled throughout the process. The more difficult type of contract is where the Customer specifies what is required as this then brings in more interfaces over the product and what is required.

Both Contracts will take the form of checking National and International standards within the contract as well as any other specifications including drawings where applicable. As the sample has already been chosen only requirements that relate to that particular product or service are examined. This is part of the sampling process.

A professional auditor will always be looking for some critical requirement. It may be a special material, tolerance or clearance or an unusual standard that is called up. From this sample he will have identified a number of specific materials that needs to be purchased and from this the controls that need to be in place to meet the specified requirements.

This in turn leads to the purchasing department, where the requisitions or standard buying descriptions can be examined within the Organisation, to again understand the specification and check that all requirements are covered in the Purchase Order to the supplier.

The process then continues to the receipt of the material and what checks, material certificates, certificates of conformity, declarations of conformity are required to verify the material is acceptable. It may even cover acceptance criteria.

It is not the intention in this guidance note to go through the whole Product Realisation process, but to give an idea of what should take place re verifying that the process does demonstrate the ability to consistently provide a product that meets customer and applicable regulatory requirement

This failure to comply with ISO 9001 2008 1.1 General Section

> **needs to demonstrate its ability to consistently provide a product that meets customer and applicable regulatory requirements.**

This is why audits have, in some areas, lost their credibility in the market place.

Part 4 Audit Criteria

Dictionary Definition:—
"Criterion" (n) a standard of judging; a rule by which opinion may be judged.
Note:—Criteria (Plural)
Audit criteria is the standard/s and/or specification/s being audited against.

ISO 9000: 2005 definition of Audit Criteria in section 3.9.3
Set of policies, **procedures (3.4.5)** or **requirements (3.1.2)** used as a reference.

The normal criteria used for quality auditing can be:—

- ISO 9001 2008
- The companies management system
    o This may be procedure/s specified by the person planning the audit
    o It may be the full system
    o It may be a particular process
- The effectiveness of the process. (Does it fulfil the purpose)
- Any other relevant standard/ legislation/requirement

Note 1:—
- The Audit Criteria should always be written down and given to the Auditor when given the audit. It should also cover the scope of the audit. The scope is important as this may and usually does restrict the Auditor to a specific process/location/area.
- The criteria is what the audit is measured against.

Note 2:—
- Auditor would need to obtain permission to go outside the scope.
- The Auditor can only link the findings to the allowable criteria

If for example the Auditor found a Financial Irregularity it would not be included in the audit report unless it could be called up against the Criteria that has been given.

Health and Safety will however always be raised but again not included in the report unless it can be raised against criteria already given.

Health and Safety is the responsibility of **ALL** personnel and must by Law be reported.

Note:—comments after someone has broken their leg "Do you know that staircase has been wet all morning you would think someone would do something!! I just knew that someone would get injured"

Legally if someone heard a person say that they could be taken to court for not reporting it as required by the Health and Safety at work Act.

Professional Auditors will be observant about all issues that help the company.

The auditor would of course mention this but not document the findings as part of their audit report if it is outside the Audit Criteria. The same would apply if the Auditor found something outside the scope of the audit this again would not form part of the report.

It would, however be important for the Auditor to report other findings where legally obliged to. It would need an extension to the scope or a modification to the audit criteria to include the area of concern within the formal report.

Part 5 Random Sample

The term "Random Sample" is regularly used by Auditors.

It is often understood to mean where the auditor takes a sample completely at random.

This is considered to be incorrect when carrying out professional audits.

Another term currently being used is "Selective or Representative Sample" which can be interpreted as an "**Intelligent** selection of **relevant** samples".

So what do we mean by this.

Professional auditors will look at the process being audited. What does the company make or do.

Secondly what is relevant to why the audit is being carried out.

Finally look at what a company has been making recently.

A good thing to do is try to do a walk around at the beginning of the audit to see what is currently taking place.

In the case of a product being made what is on the shop floor.

In the case of a service what is being actioned at present.

Take an example of a 2nd party audit. The auditor/s will look at what product or service their organisation wishes to purchase. This enables them to look for similar products that are or have been produced for another company. The auditors will then look at this sample and select a relevant Contract or Purchase Order.

One item is not a sample. So the auditor may take one or two of the above directly related jobs and then one or two others totally at random to see how robust their system is.

This mainly depends on the time allowed. A 2nd Party Audit particularly if it is a large contract may only have time to sample just one to three contracts and not necessarily go through the whole process for all of them.

Where it is a simple process the auditor may sample twenty or more.

The sample chosen is, from the auditor's point of view, a way of checking that the process is working. In doing this, the auditor wants to feel comfortable that the sample taken will give confidence that the system is working effectively.

Whether the sample is three or twenty plus is a decision for the auditor.

Take an example of a Hospital. The Auditor looks at what is being purchased and takes a random sample of 5 things. They turn out to be Paper Clips, Plastic waste bags, A4 paper, Ink jet cartridges and Light Bulbs.

Is the audit going to Add useful information regarding the primary process within the hospital? Is the audit adding value?

Please do not misunderstand, it is important to have general items within the audit however we are back to the original statement the selection should be **Intelligent** and **Relevant** and that the auditor should feel the sample chosen gives confidence that the system is working and will allow the organisation to produce products or services that meet the customers needs.

Audit evidence is the documented records seen or the information obtained which can be compared with the audit criteria.

Part 6 Audit Findings

ISO 9000: 2005 section 3.9.5 **Audit Findings**

Results of the evaluation of the collected **audit evidence (3.9.4)** against the **audit criteria (3.9.3)**

In simple terms everything found during the audit.

Audit Evidence (3.9.4)
Records (3.7.6) statements of fact or other **information (3.7.1)** which are relevant to the **Audit Criteria (3.9.3)** and verifiable
In simple terms everything found during the audit that is verifiable

The normal audit criteria used for auditing are:—

- ISO 9001 2008
- The companies management system
    o This may be procedure/s specified by the person planning the audit
    o It may be the full system
    o It may be a particular process
- The effectiveness of the process. (Does it fulfil the purpose)
- Any other relevant standard/legislation/requirement

All or some of the above should be given to the auditor or agreed with the person responsible for the audit prior to carrying out the audit.

During the Audit, Audit Evidence such as "Factual Statements", "Visual evidence" where things are seen as well as "Documented Evidence" are gathered. All these things are noted on the report (Check List) that should contain both good and bad things that are found.

The Auditor uses these notes to decide what is correct and what is not. This is then compared with the audit criteria to see if it achieves and follows the specified requirements.

It is always important for the audit to be balanced with both the good findings as well as the bad. Just reporting the bad findings is not good professional auditing. In fact audits where only the bad things are reported often defeat the objective of helping the organisation improve as the Audit is seen as a negative activity.

During the audit the auditor will note many things. Not all these things will be reported. The Findings are the evaluation of what was found compared with the Audit Criteria. This enables the Auditor to produce the formal report, including Non Conformities and Observations that have been found.

Again professional audits **ALWAYS** report positives as well as negatives. The importance of this cannot be overemphasised.

If Audits are to be welcomed throughout the Organisation they must be balanced. In all auditing there are always good things to report. When both the positive findings together with the negatives are reported the audit becomes a welcome activity as it is seen to be fair and balanced.

Part 7 Audit Evidence

Audit evidence is the documented records seen or the information obtained that can be compared with the audit criteria.

ISO 9000: 2005 section 3.9.4 Audit Evidence
Records (3.7.6) statements of fact or other **information (3.7.1) that,** are relevant to the **audit criteria (3.9.3)** and verifiable.

For example if a procedure stated that all Purchase Orders should be reviewed and signed off by the senior Buyer. Then during the audit the Auditor notices that out of the five Purchase Orders that were seen, only three had the signature of the Senior Buyer. The Buyer who had produced these orders had signed the other two. The Auditor would then make a note of which orders were actually looked at. Then raise this against the audit criteria and include the relevant procedure or the ISO 9001 2008 standard and clause as appropriate. The Purchase Order numbers are the Objective Evidence. e.g P.O 13679, 14320 (See Objective Evidence)

Audit evidence could also be where checking for a form that should be used it was found that it was no longer used. This is audit evidence in the way of information but would not be Objective Evidence because it is not possible to go back and see that particular form as it does not exist.

It can also be where on checking the stock items all items were found in the correct locations and in good condition as well as being stored in a careful practical manner. The Auditor should always write down the items actually looked at. e.g The 2 inch cast Iron valves in box E23, The 0-50 bar pressure gauges in box F 19 and the 6" Ring Type Gaskets in box E 29 were all in the correct location etc. (This is good positive reporting as this was correct)

In simple terms the Audit Evidence is all the information both good and bad that has been recorded onto the Audit Checklist or Findings. It may be Objective Evidence or something that is missing and not seen or even something the Auditor was told about. Where the Auditor is verbally advised that something required by the procedure is not done he should check it by getting confirmation from those involved before recording it onto the Checklist.

Audit Evidence should cover both the **GOOD** things that are found as well as the things that do not comply or make sense.

It is from this Audit Evidence that the Auditor will develop the Audit Findings to be presented to the Auditee and their Management at the closing meeting. It is good audit practice to comment on the good things that are found. When the findings are reported the Auditor should be comfortable in reporting where processes were seen to be working well. E.g. If the stores area was seen to be well controlled this should be mentioned during the closing meeting. When this is done the audittee never normally asks to see the evidence of what was found however, the auditor should be able to, if requested, present the evidence that was found that allows the auditor to make that statement. It should never be "I think its good" or "it appears to be working well". It either was it was not. Always remember to advise the auditee that the audit only covers a sample and that this does not mean there are no problems anywhere else.

Part 8 Competence

Dictionary Definition:—
"Competence" (n)
Ability to do a task
"Competent" (adj)
Adequate, sufficient: properly or legally qualified

Competence
Properly qualified and with the ability to carry out a task correctly

The judgement on how to ensure personnel are competent is crucial and at times can be a difficult task.

The first thing to decide and clearly define is what is required from the job that has to be done?

A job description is useful where it gives the description of the job and the capabilities required to achieve that. An example of a poor measure of competence is where the only judgement used is continuous repetition of the same activity without any evaluation of whether what was done was in fact done correctly.

An example of where to start is to define what needs to be done and what the required outcome is. This then leads to the skills and knowledge required. An example of how the Auditor can begin to identify competence is to ask personnel to confirm that they feel comfortable in doing the task assigned to them. Do they believe they have all the skills necessary to carry out the task correctly? This approach was tried many years ago with a surprising result. Equipment Inspectors who went to manufacturing plants to witness tests and inspections were asked to confirm their expertise in the areas they were being sent to work. To do this a list of generic products such as, Heat Exchangers, Vessels, Turbines, Diesel Engines, Valves, Pumps, Electric Motors etc were given to each inspector and they were asked to put:—

1. Knowledgeable
2. Satisfactory
3. Weak

This was done to ensure all personnel were comfortable with what they were being asked to do and to identify where there was limited knowledge and the skills profile could be improved.

It should be born in mind that all the inspectors were experienced and some with decades of work in inspection. The surprise came when one inspector who did most of the Pump inspection put a 3 (Three) down for pumps. On being questioned he admitted that when they did the tests and viewed the relevant charts e.g. NPSH he did not really understand what was going on and relied on the manufacturers staff to advise him if it was acceptable. He had also carried out pump inspection for another Organisation, as stated in his C.V., before joining the current Organisation. As can be seen experience did not make him competent. He was then sent on a training course at a pump manufacturers plant where he had not been acting as the inspector.

This highlights that repetition of doing a job is not a method of judging competence. In the instance above the only way this lack of knowledge would come out is when a pump failed to meet the specified requirements when it was in service and being used by the end user. This could have serious consequences.

The other problem area is where the understanding of what the task is supposed to achieve is wrong. If the organisation dealing with the competence issue does not know what is required then their method of judging competence will also be incorrect.

A classic example of this is the ISO 9001 Certification activity.

There are two schools of thought:—

1. ISO 9001 certification is about ensuring the Organisation being certified has a Quality Management System that complies with ISO 9001
2. ISO 9001 certification is about ensuring that the Organisation can meet customer, statutory and regulatory requirements relating to the product and the organisations own requirements.

This difference in requirement makes the judgment of Competence totally different for the two above requirements, as the knowledge required for one is different to the other.

The above only covers the understanding of what the auditor should be doing regarding the use of the ISO 9001 standard. The other competence requirement is, of course, a good understanding of the product or service being audited. Without this knowledge it is difficult for the auditor to add value and carry out an effective professional Audit.

There are Auditors who state they do not need to know the Product or Service as they are only auditing to see if the Management System complies with ISO 9001. As will be seen from this document this is incorrect. There is such a thing as a document review and this would be checking that the Management System covers the relevant requirements of the standard, however when actually auditing the Organisation the purpose is to ensure the Management System is capable of consistently meeting the specified requirements.

From above the view of the different Certification Body on how they measured Competence could be totally different dependent on which of the above schools of thought they accepted when judging Competence.

This could explain why the CQI has stated that Purchasing Organisations have reduced confidence in ISO 9001 Certification due to the significant variation in the Quality of Third Party Certification.

The truth is:—

ISO 9001 is a Tool not an Objective

Part 9 Declaration of Conformity (D of C)

Dictionary Definition:—
"Declaration" (n) Stating and announcing, openly and explicitly, or formally; emphatic, solemn or legal assertion or proclamation.
"Conformity" (n) Compliance with
"Liable" (adj) legally bound answerable for

Declaration of Conformity n

A legal assertion that the item provided is in compliance with the specification.

The Declaration of Conformity is one of the common threads throughout the CE marking directives.

There is a need in certain industries to provide a Declaration of Conformity for every product that is made.

This is certainly true when Organisations provide equipment that is used in Explosive Atmospheres. (ATEX). The Declaration of Conformity may be used in many different industries where it is important to verify what the product complies with.

What does this mean?

In simple terms it is to ensure that each individual product produced has a certificate signed by a responsible person in the Organisation to confirm that the actual product they have provided does comply with the specifications called up.

What is the difference between this and the Order or Contract Requirements?

It is really to identify one individual within the supplying Organisation who is legally responsible for that product complying with the specification.

There is a misconception by senior personnel that when they sign this they are only signing to say the product is verified and validated to be able to meet its approved design requirements. Unfortunately this is not so. They are signing to say that particular product made that day has been made to the approved specification. They are therefore liable should this product, for whatever reason, not meet the specified requirements in compliance with the approval given for that product.

When this is explained the first reaction is "Well I am not signing it as I don't actually make it myself". This is where a management system that is in compliance with ISO 9001 should, if applied correctly, give all the information necessary to ensure that each product does in fact comply. There are normally "Route Cards", "Check Lists", "Test Results", etc that if completed properly and traceable to the individual contract or batch number ensure that the product does comply. If the process for signing and issuing the D of C is only done when all the relevant activities within the process have been signed by the relevant Competent Personnel at each stage of the process, then, and only then, can a D of C be issued to go with the product. Obviously the person issuing the D of C must have checked that all the relevant documents have been completed and signed off by the competent personnel. The person issuing the D of C may or may not be the person who has signed the D of C. It is, however, the responsible party who verifies that all requirements have been met who is ultimately responsible but as long as each process has been signed off to be in compliance that should ensure that the responsibility is on each and every person in the process.

What should be in a Declaration of Conformity (D of C)

There should be the name and address of the Organisation that has made or put the product on the market. It should be noted that this Organisation is responsible for all issues relating to the Product and are responsible for ensuring any sub contracted activity is controlled as they cannot devolve themselves of the responsibility in any way whatsoever. It is their product and therefore their responsibility.

The D of C should then also contain the following for Atex Directive 94/9/EC:—

1. The name and identification mark and the address of the manufacturer or his authorised representative established within the Community
2. A description of the equipment, protective system, or device referred to in Article 1 (2)
3. All relevant provisions fulfilled by the equipment, protective, system, or device referred to in Article 1 (2).
4. Where appropriate, the name identification number and address of the notified body and the number of the EC-Type-examination certificate
5. Where appropriate reference to the harmonised standards.
6. Where appropriate, the standards and technical specifications which have been used
7. Where appropriate, references to other community Directives which have been applied
8. Identification of the signatory who has been empowered to enter into commitments on behalf of the manufacturer or his authorised representative established within the community.

Note:—it is impossible in a document like this to cover all requirements for all relevant bodies. Requirements can change and that is why it is important to be working with the latest Standards applicable to the Organisation.

E.G
For ATEX products Directive 94/9/EC requires.
Group II Cat 2GD Ex ed IIB T4
BASEEFA 1189 Buxton
Baseefa04ATEX1234 Latest Supplement Baseefa 04ATEX1234/3 13 Feb 2007
Baseefa 1180 Buxton UK
Harmonised Standard EN 60079-7:2003
Other Standards and Specifications:—
EN 60079-0:2004 (technically identical to EN 60079-0:2006 Harmonised

EN 50018:2000 (A review of EN 60079-1:2004 which is harmonised showed no significant changes relevant to this equipment.
EN 61241-0:2006 (State of the Art—intended for harmonisation)

This is just an example showing the type of information required to satisfy Directive 94/9/EC and the product approval requirements. These requirements can differ between regulatory bodies and it is important to check to ensure the relevant specified requirements are being met.

Part 10 Certificate of Compliance (C of C)

Dictionary Definition:—
"Certificate" (n) Document formally attesting to the fulfilment of conditions.
"Compliance" (n) Action in accordance with request, demand
"Conformity" (n) Compliance with

Certificate of Compliance/Conformity

Is a certificate that attests to the fulfilment of the specified requested requirements.

There is a need in certain industries to provide a Declaration of Conformity for every product that is made. (See Guidance Note Part 9)

There is however often a requirement for a certificate of conformity (Compliance) and this is often used for items that form part of a product.

If an Organisation requires material or machined parts to allow them to manufacture their product it is normal for them to ask for a Certificate of Conformity. (C of C).

The difference between a D of C and a C of C is that a D of C is normally what is required for a finished product where as a C of C is what is required for material bought in to make into a product. This of course varies with which country is involved and who is using the term.

The ministry of Defence has a "**C of C including traceability**". Where it is defined as:—

A declaration by the supplier to the Acquirer that, apart from any identified and approved concessions the products conform to contract requirements.

It should be recognised that often the Product requiring a D of C may also be a part put into a final completed product however the difference is that it is, by itself, a complete and functioning product.

A C of C is often a requirement of the Purchase Order where it is a critical component or part of the final product. It does not of course stop the need for Material Certificates or Test Certificates that may be deemed necessary for confirmation that the item is to specification.

It may even need formal traceability as required by the Ministry of Defence.

Whether a D of C is more legally binding than a C of C is not in the Authors ability to comment on and advice from elsewhere may be appropriate.

Part 11 Controlled Documents

What is meant by Controlled Documents?

There are two types of document in use in Quality management systems and they are "Controlled" and "Uncontrolled" Documents.

There can be a lot of confusion about what this means especially now that there are complete quality management systems all controlled on computer.

It is worth going back over the intention of having Controlled Documents when the system was just a "Hard Copy" paper system.

The ISO 9001 standard is quite specific in section 4.2.3e Control of Documents where it states controls needed to ensure that relevant versions of the applicable documents are available at point of use. This is quite easy to understand, as it is a sensible approach that allows personnel to work with the latest version of any documents. These documents are not just procedural documents but can be Drawings, Quality Plans, National and International Standards or any other document that is needed by the individual to do their job.

There have been many examples where if a copy is taken off the computer the copy is automatically identified as "Uncontrolled" only valid on day of print.

This approach is sometimes used as a method of ensuring that the system cannot be blamed if personnel use uncontrolled copies, however this is not the way to run a QMS. The QMS is supposed to work for the user not the user work for the system.

Going back to 4.2.3e above the intention of the standard is to ensure that the system controls the issue of the procedures and other QMS documents in a manner that all personnel have, at the point of use, access to the latest version of any documents they need to do their job. It is not acceptable to issue Uncontrolled Documents to personnel who need these documents on a day to day basis unless it is used that day:

e.g. a check list that is filled in at that time. If it is a procedure then this should certainly be issue controlled to those without a computer.

This use of "Uncontrolled" documents is an area that is prone to error. If personnel have printed "Uncontrolled" QMS documents off the computer and use them because they need to refer to a Hard Copy version to do their job, then those copies should be hard copy "Controlled" documents. The suggestion that it is the users responsibility to check the issue status defeats the purpose of the QMS. The system is there to ensure that each individual has the latest versions in a format that enables them to do their work.

So what does Controlled documents mean?

In simple terms it means the individual issued with the document does not have to check the documents themselves to see if the version is the latest as the system will, when a new updated document is issued, ensure they are aware of or sent a new "Controlled" copy of the document. The holder may be asked to destroy or return the old copy dependent on what the procedure for Control of Document states.

This can, in a properly controlled computerised system, ensure that the holder has the latest version because provided there is access to the computer it will be the latest version. It is unacceptable for the system to demand that the user has to confirm whether they are working to the latest version, as the system should do this.

Uncontrolled Documents

Users of uncontrolled documents know they will not be advised of any revision.

There have been many instances where personnel who do not have a computer are issued with Uncontrolled copies. This is wrong and unacceptable as uncontrolled documents are documents issued for information only.

Part 12 Certification

12.1 Why was BS 5750/ISO 9001 Certification Introduced?

The reason ISO 9001 certification was introduced was to reduce multiple assessments.

It started when one manufacturer, who was believed to be a Turbine manufacturer, stood up at a meeting called by the Government to improve the quality of British Manufacturing and explained that he could improve his efficiency if he was not audited by the buying organisations so often. On being questioned he explained that he had been audited over 40 times in one year. These audits consisted of teams of two to four personnel over two to five days. He also indicated that the Auditors were basically going over the same ground and it was this repetition that was galling.

He went on to say that he had four full time staff that did nothing but look after these auditors and it was not unusual to have two audits taking place at the same time. When this stoppage time was added together with time lost answering the auditor's questions it made a big impact on the Organisations efficiency.

12.2 Why were Purchasers carrying out Vendor Appraisal or Supplier Evaluations?

During this period, which coincided with a Major development of Offshore Fields in the U.K. sector, demand was high and it became imperative to have more information on Vendors/Suppliers. When the government introduced the Scheme, where Certification Bodies were able to be approved by an Accreditation body to carry out Audits, to ensure Organisations had Quality management Systems that enabled them to demonstrate that they could meet the specified requirements.

12.3 What are audits carried out by Certification Bodies supposed to achieve?

If the reply is "to See if the Organisations complies with the ISO 9001 2008" they are wrong if they believe it only refers to clauses 4 –8.

ISO 9001 2008 is a tool not an Objective. It is a tool for the Organisation to ensure that they have the system in place to ensure that they can consistently provide a product/service that meets the specified requirements. It is also the criteria used by the Auditors to measure whether the Organisations have the Management System Requirements, Management Responsibilities, Resource Management, Product Realisation and finally the Measurement, Analysis and Improvement in place.

An audit should enable the Organisation to demonstrate that they have a Management System that will consistently meet customer requirements by producing products/services that meet the specified requirements. It also encourages Organisations to actively look at improving the product/service as well as the processes being used.

ISO 9001 IS THE TOOL NOT THE OBJECTIVE

To do this effectively during an audit, Auditors must follow AN AUDIT TRAIL. (See Part 1 Audit Trail also IRCA Inform Audit Trail and ISO 9001 Auditing practices Group)

FINALLY as a lot of personnel who carry out training tend to major on sections 4 to 8 of the ISO standard they forget to advise students what the general requirements ISO 9001 (Section 0.1 General) clearly states:—

This International Standard can be used by anybody to assess the organisations ability to **MEET customer statutory and regulatory requirements applicable to the PRODUCT** and the organisations own requirements.

Auditors should therefore concentrate on ensuring that the Organisation has the Management System and the statutory and regulatory requirements relating to the product in place to ensure it meets the PRODUCT specified requirements.

"THIS CAN ONLY BE DONE IF AN AUDIT TRAIL IS FOLLOWED"

REMINDER
ISO 9001 2008
1.1 General Section
This International Standard specifies requirements for a quality management system where an Organisation:—

a) needs to demonstrate its ability to consistently provide a product that meets customer and applicable regulatory requirements. *(This may have been mentioned before!!!)*

Note:—The statutory and regulatory requirements called up in ISO 9001 in the Scope General Section 1.1a) only relate to the statutory and regulatory requirements that are applicable to the product.

12.0 FINAL Thoughts

1. You will have seen throughout this document the failure to follow an Audit Trail is an important reason why audits are not always effective.
2. The reason this document was developed was because the author was encouraged to put together a guidance document for auditing following the articles on "Audit Trail"
3. The author dislikes seeing a very good International Standard being misused and losing credibility due to failure to teach and understand the true purpose of ISO 9001.

It is the intention of the author to use the "Back to Basics" approach in this document to bring some credibility to ISO 9001 Certification by initiating a 3 to 5 year improvement project. This will however need relevant parties to recognise that there is a need for an Improvement Project that can bring credibility back to auditing.

Note:—

Copies of the initial proposal for the "**Improvement Project**" are available if anybody would like to see them.

It is however not in the power of the author to take this any further without support.
www.pdqms.co.uk

**WHY NOT BECOME PART OF THE SOLUTION
NOT THE PROBLEM.**

PROFESSIONAL AUDITS, BOTH INTERNAL AND EXTERNAL, CAN BE VERY EFECTIVE IN IMPROVING THE BUSINESS AND REDUCING ERROR

MAKE SURE YOUR ORGANISATION APPLIES ISO 9001 EFFECTIVELY

Appendix A

Audit Plan
Company C
17th-18th XXXX

NOTE Only the items highlighted in bold are the actual listed items in the Audit Plan

The text beneath is a simplified summary of what is carried out. This is to demonstrate how an Audit Trail may be followed. More detailed requirements follow later in this document.

Day 1
08.30 Arrival and walk around to review process
This arrival gives opportunity to review the process before the opening meeting. It also allows for any delay in arriving as the auditor can go straight to the Opening Meeting. The walk around allows current jobs to be identified and their Contract/Order Numbers to be noted. It also gives an idea of the layout of the Organisation.

09.00 Opening Meeting
No comment on this as auditors should all know the process for an Opening Meeting.

09.20 Quality Representative
This area is where the auditor can see how the Organisation manages its business.
- **Review documented system (QM/Procedures/Standards docs etc)**
Where possible the Quality Manual, together with the Document Control Procedure will have already been read before arriving at the location. The issue status and controls can be discussed together with the register for these documents indicating their status.
- **Review register of controlled documents (Inc National Int Standards etc)**

The controlled list of documents should be reviewed and controls and issues understood

- **ISO 9001 Certificates and last report/any corrective actions**

Previous reports can be reviewed to ascertain if any issues have been raised and how well they have been closed out.

- **Previous Non Conformities/Internal Audits/Management Review**

The review of these documents can often tell the auditor how well management control the Organisations systems and how effective they are.

- **Customer Complaints/Customer Feedback**

Again it is important to see how these issues are dealt with and how much information there is.

- **Identify Process (Walk around if not already done)**

All the above can, in the first hour or so, indicate how well the Organisation manages its business. It indicates how good their Internal Audits are and how effective Management Reviews are. This is an opportunity to open discussion concerning the Contract Orders that have been identified and it allows questions to be asked about those specific orders. This can help decide which of the current vehicles should be audited.

10.20 Review what vehicles are in for service.

Check on what documents are passed down to the technicians working on the vehicles. Identify service schedule documents especially those related to the vehicles already chosen and are in for service.

- Identify any customers special requirements
- Finalise samples for audit

This is the opportunity to view the management system that is used to control this activity. To see how the vehicles are booked in and scheduled. Who does this is the information available for those taking orders adequate to ensure that the work can be done in the given time frame.

Obtain any documents that relate to the selected sample of jobs going through that day.

11.00 Planning
- Review programme for chosen contracts/Purchase Orders
- Identify any special requirements

Identify how the Organisation plans the work and identifies any unusual or special requirements. The system should be able to handle standard contracts easily.

11.45 Sales
- Review customer requirements order number etc
- Identify requirements
- Review Marketing Documents/Sales Literature

This is where the detail of the actual specification for the service is chosen. It is where special or unusual requirements can be picked out. This is the start of the formal Audit Trail. It is where the auditor skills pick up on the unusual or critical requirements as well as some general requirements. This information, together with any applicable drawings, work instructions or procedures are identified. It is also gives the opportunity to see how effective their liaison with their customers is. Have they given the customer accurate information on what will be done and how much it will cost.

It is also important to ensure sales literature such as special pricing, discounts and what will be carried out is unambiguous.

12.30. Lunch

13.00 Servicing
- **Obtain and use specific check list for the different types of service that will be carried out**
- **Control of manufacturing standard service list**
- **Follow process through and check documents in use and controls**

This is where the actual servicing activity takes place it covers each vehicle and how this information is passed down to the technician doing the job.

It covers all the controls that the Organisation has put in place. It is the chance for the auditor to see what is actually done. It includes seeing the facilities and equipment utilised and the competence of the personnel. Any testing that may be carried out. Examine the records that are kept together with the "Service Cards" and how they are controlled and retained as a formal record of what was done. It gives a clear understanding of what parts were used. During this process critical items, can be identified and noted for checking within the purchasing department. Equipment used during testing is noted for checking their calibration status.

15.30. Handling and Controls
- **Identify key components and controls**
- **Any special requirements Tolerances etc**
- **Markings**

Within this servicing area specific interest is noted of the handling and controls that are in place. It should be born in mind that this is customer property and must be looked after carefully. This covers tolerances, special processes such as welding, electronic testing equipment, judging when an item is no longer suitable and needs to be renewed and getting customer agreement before carrying out unscheduled work. e.g. Brake Pads. How is extra work managed regarding the time needed to do the work.

16.30. Review Findings and Feed back
This is an opportunity to identify what has been found, both good and of concern. This allows confirmation by the guide. Any concerns identified during the audit would have been advised to the guide at that time but may need clarification.

17.15 Close for day one

Day 2
Note it is always good practice to go over the findings in detail overnight. To ensure all Audit Evidence is reviewed and highlight any further clarification that may be needed.

08.15 Arrival
General discussion. (Progress to date)

08.45 Purchasing
Identify key components and controls

- Review Approved Supplier List (ASL)
- Identify Critical Suppliers
- C of C required (See guidance Documents 10)
- Review controls within Purchase Order.
- Any special requirements Tolerances etc

This is another critical area because if the basic raw materials have not been correctly specified and obtained it is impossible to carry out a service that would comply with the manufacturers warranty.

From the items seen in the service area various items will have been identified and the method of ensuring they do meet the required specification should be examined. Are only manufacturers parts the only parts that are allowed to be used. This includes making sure all special requirements regarding Material Specification, Testing, Certification and any special processes needing control are specified in the Purchase Order.

10.00 Goods Receiving and Stores
- Materials receipt
- Storage and control (Any Special needs)
- Issue of items to production
- Control of stock (FIFO)
- Condition of stock
- Control and Marking of products before despatch

This is where the purchased material is received and controlled. It is where the received material is held prior to use by the technicians and must be held in a manner that enables, where required, traceability can be ensured. FIFO first in first out could be a positive way of ensuring material is not kept on the shelf until it is unusable.

11.15. Review final completion process and return of vehicle to the customer.
- Review procedures/instructions
- Review completed documents

- How any additional activities have been cleared with the client
- Is the vehicle clean and in good order
- Review hand over to customer
- What information is given to the customer and what documents are handed over to the customer indicating what was carried out.

This is where the Auditor ensures the service has been carried out effectively and all activities have been recorded and passed to the customer prior to final payment and release.

12.00. Training records/Competencies
- **Sample staff and see records, confirm competences**

The important thing regarding following an audit trail is to check on personnel seen during the audit and verify that the records held on them as individuals ensures that they were capable of doing the jobs they were seen doing. Use selective sampling of activities seen.

12.30 Lunch

13.15 Review improvement situation statisticsDespatch
- **Management Responsibility**
- **Control and Marking of products before despatch**
- **Responsibility for despatch**

This is the area where the product is finally despatched. Who is responsible, is there a C of C or a D of C (See Guidance Notes Parts 9 and 10)

13.45 Documentation and Records
- **Retention recall and condition**

All Contract requirements must be met to ensure a satisfactory conclusion to the Contract. It could include sending the correct documents, certificates, operating information etc. How is this Despatch recorded how would a recall work if necessary.

14.15 Revisit areas for clarification (If required)
- **Review Audit evidence and develop findings and prepare report**

15.45 Closing Meeting
This is where the auditor has the opportunity to advise the Auditee of the Findings. It is normal for auditors to identify where processes are well controlled and report these good areas first. If auditing is seen to be beneficial then it has to be a balanced audit. Audits that only discuss the non—conformities and concerns are not professional audits.

16.15 Questions discussion

16.30 Close

Appendix B

KEY HIGHLIGHTS

KEY 1: REMEMBER ISO 9001 IS THE TOOL NOT THE OBJECTIVE

KEY 2:—*All audits should give the audited Organisation information about how robust their systems are in ensuring that they can consistently meet the required specification.*

KEY 3:—*It has been accepted that some Purchasing Organisations have reduced confidence in ISO 9001 Certification.*

KEY 4:—*The Statutory and Regulatory requirements called up in ISO 9001 clause 1.1a) are only those requirements that relate to the product/service itself.*

KEY 5:—*There is still a belief that certification audits are to see if the ISO 9001 Clause 4-8, are covered within the organizations management system. This is incorrect as it conveys little or no information on how effective the processes are.*

KEY 6:—*From the above it is obvious that all auditing is about ensuring that the organisation can consistently meet the specified requirements.*

KEY 7:—*The failure to carry out a <u>process</u> audit following an <u>audit trail</u> is the single most important reason why audits are not effective*

KEY 8:—*AUDIT TRAIL: (Draft as no agreement has been reached) An examination, by a qualified person, of an activity following the path that has been left by the process*
OR
A systematic approach to collecting evidence based on specific samples, that the output of a series of inter-related processes meets expected outcomes (APG version)

KEY 9:—When auditing against ISO 9001 it is not the clauses that are being audited but the process.

KEY 10:—From above it should be obvious that the purpose of the audit is to ensure that the Management System is adequate to ensure that each process throughout the system is able to consistently achieve and meet the required outputs.

KEY 11: It is important to remember that selected contract requirements are being audited to see if they have been effectively dealt with and are being met. This is why the auditor must know what the contract says and take a selective sample of those requirements to see if the processes are properly controlled.

KEY 12: It is important throughout the audit to ask each auditee what procedures, instructions, check lists, forms etc they work to and note whether these are the latest version and are Controlled or Uncontrolled documents. (ISO 9001 2008 Ref 4.2.3d) The use of Uncontrolled documents at the point of use are not normally acceptable unless they are used on the day of issue.

KEY 13: It is important that having identified National or International standards that are called up in the Contract that the method of ensuring they are working to the latest version is effective. Does the contract identify the applicable version? Does the system in place have access to the latest issues?

KEY 14:—ISO 9001 allows exclusions from clause 7.0 Product Realisation Process where they do not affect the products ability to consistently meet the specified requirements. Other clauses apply but as appropriate to the Organisations business

KEY 15:—It is important that the auditor understands the requirements of the requisition and ensures these requirements match the specification from the contract.

KEY 16:—It is, at this point, important to remind auditors how essential it is to gather audit evidence (ISO 9000 3.9.4) of what was seen.

(Guidance Note Part 7)

KEY 16A Audit Evidence leads to Audit Findings that in turn leads to Audit Conclusions. This once again highlights the importance of a common understanding being achieved by using the ISO 9000 definitions.

KEY 17:—Always follow the chosen Audit Trail as it is too easy for auditors to take samples at different stages of the process that are not related or linked to the sample/s chosen. This only allows the auditor to be able to check if a document is filled in correctly, missing out on being able to verify that the process is actually working.

KEY 18:—The importance of starting the service with the correct spares for the parts being changed is paramount as using the wrong material would ensure the service did not meet specification. It should be noted any change in material must have formal approval.

Note:—Although not relevant to this example but important to auditing in general the use of the so called 'better' grade of material without design change justification and approval is never acceptable.

KEY 19 Auditing of the process would entail physically reviewing what is taking place by sampling specific items and witnessing any tolerances required such as "Torque settings" for head tightening. Auditing is not just a paper exercise.

KEY 20:—Auditing of a process must follow an audit trail or it is impossible to verify that requirements are being met.

KEY 21 The term "CAPA" should NOT be used to link the terms Corrective Action (CA) and Preventative Action (PA as they are not related when being used in ISO 9001.

KEY 22:—It is important to follow the same item throughout the activity to verify that the process is controlled and could ensure that the full specification was achieved each time.

KEY 23
A quality audit does not indicate that the product itself is suitable for what it will be used for just that the organisation can consistently make the product to the specified requirements.

KEY 24 Auditors should have some knowledge and competence in the product or service being carried out. This then enables them to accept that procedures and work instructions etc may not be necessary where competent personnel are being used.

KEY 25:—It is not the Audit Trail of the procedure that is followed but the Audit Trail of the process.

KEY 26:—In the closing meeting the Organisation would be advised that the audit was by sampling and that because nothing had been identified as being wrong it does not mean there was nothing wrong.

KEY 27:—Some auditors spend more time ensuring each element of the ISO 9001 Standard has a "Tick" against it than ensuring the system is effective.

KEY 28:—Professional Auditing is NOT about seeing if the management system complies with ISO 9001 clause 4-8 but seeing that the system used within that Organisation is capable of consistently achieving the intended outcome.

This can only be done if you follow an Audit Trail.

ISO 9000 Family of Standards
with extracts for
ISO 9001 Audit Trail (First edition)

Appendix C

INDEX

Page	Section	Description
1		Index
2	1.0	Introduction
2	2.0	Scope
3	3.0	Summary
5	4.0	ISO 9000 Fundamentals and Vocabulary
13	5.0	ISO 9001 QMS Requirements
30	6.0	ISO 9004 Manage for sustained success
38	7.0	ISO 19011 Guidelines auditing management systems
44	8.0	Conclusions
45	9.0	Final Thoughts
46	APPENDIX A	Other Related Quality Standards
48	APPENDIX B	ISO 9001 Auditing Practices Group (Audit Trail)
51	APPENDIX C	5 Year Improvement Plan
53	APPENDIX D	Key Points
55	APPENDIX E	ISO 9001 Audit Trail March 2010 (extracts)
77		Audit Trail Appendix A

QUICK TIP:—
Knowing how busy people are I recommend that for a quick read concentrate on the BOLD TEXT only and you will quickly pick up the messages within the book. Then if you require more detailed information please read the adjacent text.

ISO 9000 Family of Standards

1.0 Introduction

There is a considerable difference of opinion as to what the ISO 9000 Family of Standards (FoS) consists of and how the documents should be used.

They are a set of generic standards of immense benefit to business because they can help any organisation to manage, control, and improve their business. Most organisations are aware of ISO 9001 however there is a lot of misunderstanding about how ISO 9001 should be used and many companies do not even have ISO 9000 or know about ISO 9004. It should be noted that ISO 9000, 9001 and 9004 are a set of standards that are able to support any types of organisation. Unfortunately not many Organisations are aware of the benefits hence the reason for this document.

This book is an attempt to help Organisations choose the standards that are most applicable to their business from the ISO 9000 Family of Standards (FoS)

2.0 Scope

The scope of this document is identified in ISO 9000 where it defines the ISO 9000 Family of Standards (FoS) as:—

ISO 9000 Quality management systems—Fundamentals and vocabulary

This describes the fundamentals and specifies the terminology for quality management systems.

ISO 9001 Quality management systems requirements

This specifies requirements for a quality management system where an organisation needs to demonstrate its ability to provide products that not only fulfil customer and applicable regulatory requirements but also enhances customer satisfaction.

ISO 9004 Managing for the sustained success of an organisation—A quality management approach

This provides guidelines that consider both the effectiveness and efficiency of the quality management system. The aim of this standard is improvement in the performance of the organisation and increased satisfaction of customers and other interested parties.

ISO 19011 Guidelines for auditing management systems

This strictly speaking is a support document applicable to organisations that carry out audits of management systems. It focuses, in particular, upon the competence of those involved in carring out audits and how they control and manage this activity.

Note 1:—**Authors comment**: ISO 19011, although identified as part of the family, it is in fact a document that guides auditors, organisations and certification bodies in the correct control and application of auditing. In its latest issue 2011 it has gone from guidance on environmental and quality audits (2002) to cover a much broader range of auditing activity (2011).

Note 2:—It is not the intention of this document to go through all the relevant clauses in each standard but to take samples to help illustrate the purpose of each standard.

Note 3:—The purpose of this book is to make interested parties aware of how to use the ISO 9001 Family of Standards and hopefully **improve the standard of auditing**.

3.0 Summary

There are just four documents in the ISO 9000 Family of Standards (FoS) and each has a different purpose. It is the author's opinion that not fully understanding the purpose and roles of the ISO 9000

(FoS) is the principal reason why ISO 9001, the most commonly used standard, is often misunderstood.

ISO 9000 sets the ground rules and covers the terminology that should be used. It has a pivotal role within the four standards and it is designed to support the other three documents within the family to help any type of organisation manage its business in the most effective manner. It covers the eight management principles developed from the "Vision 2000" findings. It includes the basic fundamentals of a quality management system including the common terms and definitions used in quality.

ISO 9000 is the "backbone" to the "Family of Standards". As such it is important that each standard in the Family should, in their section "Normative References", refer to ISO 9000 as being an applicable reference.

ISO 9001 has a restrictive role, it enables an organisation to demonstrate its ability to consistently provide products that meets customer needs and applicable statutory and regulatory requirements. It covers agreeing with the customer what they require (Specification), then ensuring the process is planned and managed to ensure those requirements will be met. It should be noted that the statutory and regulatory requirements are only those that relate to that **product** and it is not every statutory and regulatory requirement that an Organisation has to deal with. There are many misunderstandings about ISO 9001 and some of these are covered in this book.

In many cases auditors are still being taught to see if the organisations management system has covered all the clauses 4-8 in ISO 9001. This stems from what was called the Document Review where an organisation's Quality Manual is examined to see if it has recognised and addressed all the requirements of ISO 9001 in principle. This "desktop" stage 1 audit is a specific training element from a Lead Auditor Course. It should be recognised that the Quality Manual is just a stated intent nothing more. It is a commitment explaining "WHAT" an Organisation does. It does not have to cover Why, When, How, Where and Who. The true situation is only revealed, at the levels below the Quality Manual, when a professional **process audit** is carried out to ascertain if the processes that have been put in place can consistently achieve the specified requirements. **How can an auditor ascertain if the process is able to consistently meet the specified requirements if they do not know what the specification for the product is?**

ISO 9001 has a restrictive purpose and that is to ensure that the Organisation has a management system that can consistently meet the customer's requirements. It is restricted to the process from enquiry through to delivery of the product. Certification to ISO 9001 is intended to give the Customer confidence that the management system employed by the Organisation can be relied upon to consistently meet the specified requirements.

ISO 9004 is the standard that covers the other requirements that an Organisation has to manage, that have not been addressed by the ISO 9001 standard. It includes "Risk and Strategy" and the whole purpose of ISO 9004, as stated in the title, is managing for the sustained success of an organisation. In other words it covers all the issues outside the scope of ISO 9001 that could affect an organisation's ability to be successful. This is why the whole ISO 9000 Family of Standards (FoS) should be taught, not just ISO 9001.

ISO 9004 is the final part of the Trilogy of standards that enables any Organisation to address the broader quality management issues relating to the sustained success of their business. Where ISO 9001 finishes ISO 9004 fills the gap as it provides a much wider focus on quality management than ISO 9001.

Finally ISO 19011 are the guidelines for auditing management systems. This was previously just for quality and environmental management systems (2002) but the new ISO 19011 (2011) is generic and suitable for many of the other management system standards that have been published. This standard gives guidance to the auditing activities related to management systems. It emphasises the need to conduct process audits, yet this is still misunderstood in many quarters.

ISO 19011:2011 actually illustrates how things can go wrong when standards are expanded to include other issues. ISO 19011 attempts to cover a much broader range of auditing. In doing this, the original purpose has been lost. This is illustrated by the fact that it states that no Normative References are cited. In other words ISO 9000 is no longer applicable. In this statement alone it has excluded itself from the ISO 9000 Family of Standards.

The four standards (FoS) are all explained with specific examples of how and where they may be utilised and gives organisations an opportunity to decide what stage they are at and which of the four standards are most applicable to their business.

The book itself is an attempt to identify how the ISO 9000 Family of standards should be used. It identifies some examples of incorrect use and common mistakes made in the interpretation of these standards, in particular ISO 9001. As the author does not wish to imply criticism of what is an excellent Family of Standards he has identified a 5 Year Improvement Plan that could help quality regain credibility by using the standards correctly. (See Appendix C) Revising a standard on the grounds of improvement when the standards are not used correctly is counterproductive.

The approach taken with ISO 19011 gives concern over the approach that could be taken over the ISO 9000 and ISO 9001 revision due 2014? This continual drive to add issues that should reside in ISO 9004 into ISO 9001 will, if implemented, undermine the whole ISO 9000 Family of Standards and is one of the reasons for this book.

I don't expect all readers to agree with all the views in this book, however, I would request that this book is read with an "Open Mind" leaving preconceived views to one side. I will leave the reader to decide if any of the views and proposals within this document could or should be implemented.

Note:—
The Book on the "ISO 9000 Family of Standards" is available in book or e'book format.

About the Author

David John Seear C.Eng CMarEng FIMarEST FCQI CQP is a Chartered Engineer who spent 12 years at sea ending up as Chief Engineer with a combined First Class Chief Engineers certificate before leaving and joining Shell. He left Shell U.K after 20 years service where he had been Head Of Quality and Performance for Shell UK Materials. One of the departments reporting to him was Quality Appraisal whose purpose was to carry out 2nd party audits for Shell UK and Shell den Hague. He represented the CBI on BSI QMS 22 for 6 years and represented the U.K. on ISO 9000 TC 176 for 3 years. He was a member of the Standards Development Group (SDG) in the U.K and attempted to encourage the SDG to justify the changes against the scope of the standard under review. Some recent changes to quality standards had no real justification for the changes that had been made. In fact some recent changes are now seen to be counterproductive.

He has lived in Brunei and Abu Dhabi and carried out Audits and/or Training throughout the world including Africa, North and South America, Russia as well as the areas lived in namely the Far East (e.g. Singapore, Malaysia, Brunei) and was the regional manager for a Certification Body based in the Middle East working in UAE, Kuwait, Qatar, Bahrain to name just a few of the countries he was responsible for. He is an IRCA Principal Auditor of 25 years experience and runs PDQ Management Services that carries out Training, Auditing, Consultancy and Lecturing on various management issues including procurement and Improving Management Systems. **email daveseear@btinternet.com**

www.ingramcontent.com/pod-product-compliance
Lightning Source LLC
Chambersburg PA
CBHW030818180526
45163CB00003B/1344